THE MIDDLETON STRAIN OF WORKING TERRIER

Wilkinson's Rock (By Mike Frain)

SEÁN FRAIN
IN COMPANY WITH GARY MIDDLETON

GW00683452

PENNINE PUBLISHING

First published in the UK in 2006 by Pennine Publishing

ISBN: 0-9552389-0-0
From 1/1/07 ISBN: 978-0-9552389-0-1

Dedicated to the memory of Sid Wilkinson and Anthony Barker – breeders of wonderfully game terriers.

Acknowledgements: Thanks to Gary Middleton who painstakingly guided my research and to Ruth Middleton for her hospitality and support of this project. I must also thank my wife, Glynis Frain, for her contribution, especially the back cover photo. Thanks to Pauline Middleton for providing a few photographs and also to Bob and Ruth Arnold. Thanks to Wayne Hill, Chipper Smith and Kenny McCallister, and to Barry Wild, for their help with information and photos, as well as my brother, Mike, for the drawing of Rock. Thankyou to Eddie Pool and Diane and Sheila Barker for their invaluable assistance.

All references to badger digging are from an era when this practise was considered legal and respectable. This book clearly differentiates between badger digging and badger baiting and the author and publishers wish to make it clear that they do not condone baiting of any form, nor do they encourage any to engage in the now illegal activity of badger digging, though this practise still remains legal in some countries.

CONTENTS

Bloodlines and Photo captions are found on Page 175 (some photographs are of poor quality, but have been included because they are a vital part of this record).

Introduction

The meet of the Lunesdale Foxhounds was at Brigsteer in South Cumbria and it wasn't long before they had roused a fox from its daytime hideout among the undergrowth that grows in profusion in this hilly, rather than mountainous, country. John Nicholson was Huntsman then and he had cheered his pack on as they picked up the line of their quarry and hunted it keenly across the rough and rocky ground. The morning was grey and the air rather chilly, but the followers were soon sweating as they followed in the wake of the fast-paced pack of fellhounds, their music swelling until it echoed around the hills and woodlands of this area, finally dying away as it chased across the huge swell of land towards the high peaks of the distant mountains.

The fox took them across open country and into woodland and, finally, at Brigsteer Woods, went to ground. The Huntsman was soon up with his hounds and he found a young man sitting by the rock earth into which the fox had crept, his black and tan terrier keen to get to ground in search of its foe. The young man had even beat the hounds to the earth and so he was sure he would be allowed to loose his terrier into the rocky laybrinth, but 'Nic' asked him to keep the terrier shackled, for he wanted the fox bolted and this particular earth dog had a reputation as a hard fox killer- hence the reason why he was not allowed to use it in this instance. In the springtime, when foxes often kill, or maim, lambs, a terrier with this sort of disposition is unbeatable and, indeed, highly desirable. Also, the landowner may require the fox to be killed at the earliest opportunity, not wishing to allow it too many chances at escape, for one reason or another; usually because he, or she, has had severe problems with fox predation among their livestock. Otherwise, a fox will usually be bolted in order that the hunt can carry on, in the hopes that hounds will account for their quarry above ground.

The Huntsman desired the fox to be bolted and so the young man was forced to wait patiently while a fell-type terrier was tried. After five minutes, however, the terrier had emerged, having been bitten. A second fell terrier was tried and, again, emerged after only a few minutes of work, which was unusual, for these terriers had worked with the Lunesdale pack on earlier occasions and they had proven game to fox. Turning to the young man, whose terrier was doing cartwheels on the end of its lead, 'Nic' now asked him to try his terrier and so he loosed it and it was gone in seconds, keen to get on with the job in hand. It was then that all hell broke loose and it soon became obvious that the fox was not going to bolt. Digging operations began and an assault made on this bad and difficult rock earth, the terrier screaming with rage as it worked below.

The going was hard and slow and quite a bit of rock was shifted out of that earth before, at last, the terrier was reached. Two badgers were at the hole-end and the terrier was grappling with both of them, courageously standing its ground and not allowing any of the two 'brocks' to move on elsewhere. After some time and effort, the badgers were reached and pulled out of the earth and then the fox was found. It was already dead and must have suffocated as the three other inhabitants of that narrow chamber battled it out, or maybe it had a weak heart and the goings on had proven too much for it. Whatever the reason, that young man had, in the end, been able to use his working terrier and it had not let him down. In fact, the terrier, as well as the strain it belonged to, cemented its reputation even more.

The young man in question was Gary Middleton of Kendal and the black and tan terrier he had out with him that day was Chip; a terrier from a strain of working Lakeland terriers Gary had begun a few years earlier. The reputation of this strain was growing by the day up in the Lake District, and, indeed, throughout the country, for they were proving extremely game workers, at fox and badger, and also looked as well as they worked, for they were winning at working terrier shows throughout Cumbria and beyond. In fact, Chip had won many shows by this time, but he was an even better worker, being a famous fox-killing terrier that allowed few to bolt.

This is the strain of terrier we will learn more about as we progress through this book and, believe me, this will be of great interest to any who have even a slight interest in our working terrier breeds. Gary Middleton, over the more than fifty years he has been breeding, working and showing Lakeland terriers, has made a massive contribution to the modern working terrier scene and few earth dogs today do not have at least some of the bloodlines of his dogs running in their veins.

Chip, looker and worker, the subject of our introduction.

Rusty, a Middleton bred Lakeland and Sire of Chad.

A son of Chad.

A son of Toby.

Chapter One

THE STRAIN BEGINS

The young Gary Middleton grew up with terriers and it was his Great Uncle who influenced his early ideas regarding earth dogs. He farmed around Dent, which is not far from Kendal where Gary was born and raised, and he kept and bred a strain of rough coated Fell-type terriers which were rather nondescript. These terriers, Gary states, were game working dogs, but they were not typey in the least, doing badly even at small agricultural shows. As working terriers, however, they were ideal for the purpose for which his Great Uncle kept them; for keeping down vermin around his upland farm.

The Lunesdale Foxhounds have hunted this area for quite a number of decades now and they are charged with controlling fox numbers up on these wild Cumbrian and Yorkshire fells, but they cover a large area and so some places only get hunted maybe two or three times during the season. And so quite a number of hill farmers kept a terrier or two around the place in order to deal with any predators which began attacking their livestock. Gary's Great Uncle would keep rats down on his farm and he would also use these terriers for ridding the place of unwanted residents such as foxes and badgers, which can cause serious problems when they turn to attacking stock such as chickens, geese and lambs.

These terriers, although unsuited to the show ring, were ideal for vermin control and they were suited to the area they hunted. They had wirey, rough jackets, which helped keep much of the cold at bay. This is essential in these upland areas where temperatures can suddenly drop below freezing. A terrier working a drain, or a rockpile, is in serious danger in such places and a dense coat is absolutely vital. The coats on this strain of working terrier were certainly dense, but they were far from perfect and the young Middleton was not happy with such jackets even in those early days. True, the coats offered much protection against the elements and the terrier strain was certainly hardy, having been bred in this area for many years, but Gary states that there was a certain amount of Bedlington terrier blood in the makeup of his Uncle's strain and that this influence caused the jackets to be more on the open, rather than the tight-knit, side, and that this made them vulnerable to heavy rain. That heavy rain, coupled with freezing temperatures and icy winds gusting strong enough to blow you off your feet, meant that these terriers suffered at times and Gary deemed it necessary to improve this situation as soon as he could find the most suitable stud dog for that purpose. Anyone who has hunted around Dent, or, indeed, any of the Cumbrian and North Yorkshire fells, will understand why coat type was so important to many of the older generation of fell-hunters who often found themselves still digging down to terriers as the sun sank behind the hills. In the old days, many hunts ended with a fox going to ground during the late afternoon and refusing to bolt. In this situation, a dig was always on the cards and this was carried out using lanterns placed around the earth, in much the same manner as early earth-stoppers operated. Many indeed, are the digs that have been conducted through the night in such places as North Yorkshire and Cumbria, especially up on the fells, and a terrier needs maximum protection in such hostile environments. Hence the reason for a top quality jacket being required on the future terriers of Gary Middleton.

These terriers of Gary's Great Uncle were certainly game, but they tended to be baying terriers, rather than fox killers. The strain certainly produced fox killing dogs, but these were the exception, rather than the rule, and this did not suit the young would-be terrierman, for Gary has always believed in the traditional values that shaped working terriers in Cumbria – that they should be capable of killing a fox should it refuse to bolt. This was essential for the dog terriers, but the bitches were required to bay at, rather than kill, foxes, due to their more 'delicate' nature.

Most of the terriers, including the males, from this old Dent strain were baying types and, although this suited the farmers who were happy to bolt most foxes and either shoot them, or catch them with dogs, very often farm Collies, only digging foxes out that could be dug, such as those found in dug-out rabbit holes, or drains, it meant that any fox which would not bolt from a borran earth, or maybe a man-made rockpile inside an old quarry, would have to be left to run for another day and this, Gary believes, is not acceptable to a fell-hunter, who must account for problem foxes. This is where the fox killing terrier comes into its own. Most Northern hunts have a fox killing terrier in kennel, just for such occasions when a lamb killing fox is laid up in a bad spot and will not shift, no matter how vociferous the terrier entered to it.

The landscape of the Lake District and North Yorkshire has dictated the type of terrier that has been created in these harsh landscapes over centuries and a fox killer is essential. Baying terriers also play a large part in fox control up in the fell country and a particularly vociferous terrier will succeed in shifting many foxes that would otherwise stay put. True, a terrier that stands two feet away from its foe and barks at it from a safe distance will have very little success when it comes to bolting foxes to hounds from these upland earths, but one which works its quarry hard, baying right into its face and nipping and teasing constantly, without letting-up on the pressure, will find success even in some of the most impregnable fortress earths. Hardasty's famous Turk was just such a terrier. Harry Hardasty hunted the Melbreak Foxhounds for many seasons and one of his best terriers was Turk. He was no fox killer, but he was a superb finder and could shift foxes from the deepest of borrans, for he worked his quarry hard and without letup, never giving an inch until the pressure proved too much and the fox, even though it may have been hard-pressed by hounds, would soon bolt and make for open country once more. Such was Turk's worth that, at one time, the majority of terriers found in the Western Lakes country were sired by him and his blood still runs strong even today, among working terriers found throughout the country. Even Frank Buck and Cyril Breay brought Turk's bloodlines into their strain, after Max, Frank's son, had taken one of his bitches to be mated by Turk (see *The Patterdale Terrier*, Seán Frain, published by Swan Hill Press). Brian Nuttall told me that Turk was incredibly noisy at work and that he could be heard in the deepest of earths. This makes any terrier a real asset to a Huntsman of the fell country.

The Dent strain of rough and ready terrier were certainly game and worked their foxes hard, but the young Middleton wanted a more traditional type and his search for a suitable stud dog began. In the meantime, he worked his small team of terriers obtained from his Great Uncle and enjoyed hunting rats and water voles on the river Kent. Gary was only around ten years old when he first began hunting the river with his first terrier, Tiny. Another terrier was Floss, a blue Bedlington type of Fell terrier, which he worked alongside his friend's Alsation. They would hunt the river two or three times a week and often went to a place known as 'Goose Holme' where literally hundreds of water voles could be found scurrying around under the grasses.

The terrier and Alsation would account for quite a number before the voles would slip into the water and make good their escape. Indeed, during some evenings they took as many as 100 voles with their two dogs. Water voles, of course, are now becoming more scarce due to mink predation in the main and it is illegal to hunt them now anyway (and rightly so!), but things were different back then. They were found on all waterways in abundance and the activities of the two young lads didn't even seem to put a dent in the population. Gary found these early terriers from his Great Uncle's strain to be ideal workers for such tasks and they eagerly busied themselves with hunting the waterways for rats and any other huntable creatures they came across.

The Dent terriers were of a handy size for work, but, in the main, were a little too fine in the bone for Middleton's liking, having quite small heads and snipey jaws. Not that these do not make good and very useful workers. Gary has seen quite a few useful fox killing terriers with slight heads and he does not decry ones of this type. Indeed, he remembers a terrier owned by Malcolm Lambert that was death to any fox. This was a little red dog named Jack and he was only slight of head, yet he could kill foxes very quickly indeed. Still, Gary prefers a good strong head on a terrier and the stud dog he sought for outcross blood must have such a head if he was to use it on his bitches. Meanwhile, Gary continued working his Dent terriers with considerable success, taking foxes, badgers and rats with them, whenever the opportunity arose.

A few years after starting with working terriers and now having some experience under his belt, Middleton began his search for a suitable stud dog and there were quite a number available to him at that time; terriers that not only looked good, but worked even better, serving at the hunt kennels of local fell packs on a regular basis. Hardasty's Turk was one of these and Gary does not question the abilities of this grand working terrier, but at the time of Turk's prime there was much controversy over his breeding and Gary wanted a stud dog of certain ancestry. Also, Turk was no fox killer and he did not have the powerful head Middleton was searching for, in order to improve bone in the Dent strain.

It was around this time that Gary began forging a friendship with Anthony Barker and Sid Wilkinson of Patterdale and Glenridding and he learnt much from these two well-known hunting figures. Barker had a long association with hounds and working terriers and his experience was equalled by very few.

He was the son of Fred Barker who hunted the Pennine pack of Foxhounds from Ousby where he farmed sheep among the edges of the wild Northern Pennines, finally moving to Patterdale during the early 1920s. Fred Barker bred his own strain of terrier, based on 'Chowt-faced' Rock and two white-bodied terriers from a southern badger digging club, with whom Barker traded terriers when outcross blood was necessary. Rock was an incredibly game terrier who saw much service with both the Pennine Foxhounds and the Ullswater Foxhounds, and undoubtedly the Carlisle and District Otterhounds too, whenever they hunted the Ullswater country during the summer months. Rock was not only a superb worker, even among some of the roughest and wildest country imaginable, where nightmare earths abound, but he was also a very fruitful sire of workers. He not only produced top quality fox, badger and otter dogs, but also put good bone and head into his offspring – a trait that continued to bear fruit several generations down the line. Also, like himself, Rock produced fox killers that were capable of doing the job without receiving too much damage. True, after several seasons of such work, and some terriers serve with the fell packs for as many as ten or eleven seasons (though harder terriers tend to have a shorter working life), they inevitably become battle-scarred, but usually come out of encounters with fox without too much damage from each encounter. And, like much of Bowman's stuff, a strain Rock was reputedly descended from, he produced offspring that were capable of killing as many as three foxes in one day's hunting – an incredible feat for any working terrier.

One of Rock's most famous descendants was Anthony Barker's Rock, also known as 'Chowt-faced' Rock, and this terrier was an incredibly game worker to fox, being one of those that could kill up to three foxes in one day's hunting. Even in old age, Rock killed foxes almost casually and on more than one occasion he was used to finish foxes that were proving too much for other hunt terriers (see *The Fell Terrier*, D. Brian Plummer, the section on Anthony Barker). Barker's Rock had just died when Middleton began associating with Anthony Barker and Sid Wilk's, but there were quite a number of his progeny still around at the time and Gary was sure that this strain of terrier was the most suitable for improving his Dent strain of earth dogs.

Not only was the Barker strain incredibly game, producing consistently good, and sometimes great, workers; traditional fox killers among the males, and sometimes even the females, but good coats and bone was also consistently produced in this line. Fred and Anthony Barker rated good coat highly among their workers and for good reason.

Global warming had not affected the elements in anyway during their heydays and the winters were long and often ice cold. The Lake District is rather a wet place for much of the time and it is rain, coupled with icy winds, that has the worst effects on working terriers. True, the fell hounds are out in all weathers and they only have short coats, but hounds, apart from when they are stood around waiting for a fox to bolt, are usually on the go all the time and expend that much energy that they simply do not feel the cold. Indeed, hounds that go out with ample weight in a morning, will return to kennels with not an ounce of fat on them and they will require a good feed or two in order to get their weight back up to normal. It is very different for terriers. They are generally coupled and follow in the wake of the Huntsman. He will often be stood on a mountain top watching his hounds work and so terriers will sometimes spend a lot of time standing around. Also, when a fox is to ground, those not employed below will be stood about outside an earth and they do suffer whilst doing so, even those with the best of jackets. Hence the reason why the Barker's always bred with the aim of producing top quality jackets on their strain of terrier. The only trouble was, Fell terriers have been bred down from Bedlington terriers and so more open coats are common. In fact, during the hunting season when jackets are not stripped out, they often grow long and more open and this betrays their Bedlington ancestry. Thankfully, with stripping, a much harsher and tighter coat can be obtained and, done at the correct time, will remain as such for much of the winter (more about stripping jackets in another chapter).

Although there has been much controversy surrounding the origins of Fell and Lakeland terriers and which breeds went into the mix, I think it is now unquestionable that Irish terrier has played a massive part in the development of these strains. Cumbria and North Yorkshire have a long association with Irish farm labourers who, for at least the last couple of centuries, have travelled to these shores in order to find seasonal work. And it is reasonable to suggest that these brought their Irish breeds of terrier with them, maybe even trading them and taking early Fell types back with them to their native soil.

Irish terriers were not unknown on English shores even during the eighteenth century when a young Irishman travelled from Manchester to the Lake District, where he intended enjoying a holiday walking among the vast swell of majestic mountains. Tragically, he fell to his death from Striding Edge which winds precariously across Helvellyn, his Irish terrier climbing down to where his body lay undiscovered for the next three months. Wordsworth wrote a poem commemorating the event and he romanticised the loyalty of the dog, which had stuck with its master for so long.

'Fidelity' is the title of the poem and Wordsworth waxes lyrical about the unusual event. He tells of how a shepherd is alerted by a dog and of how it leads him to the spot where he '…found, a human skeleton on the ground.'

The shepherd then remembered that he had seen the walker three months before, setting off in the direction of Helvellyn where the tragedy occurred. And then comes the celebration of the loyalty of his faithful dog. 'This dog, had been through three months' space, a dweller in that savage place...' '...since the day, when this ill-fated traveller died, the dog had watched about the spot, or by his master's side...' There was little true romance in this event, however, for the skeleton revealed what had really occurred. The bones were stripped of every sinew and some were gnawed. The dog was in great shape, despite three months out on the mountain, being obviously well nourished. The Irish terrier, finding itself alone, had obviously lived off the meat of its master until it was at last discovered three months after the fatal fall! A particularly gruesome, rather than romantic, tale!

While there may have been much controversy over the use of breeds such as Irish terriers among many enthusiasts of the British Isles, there has been little controversy within the Lakes country itself, for I have found that it is common knowledge that Irish settlers brought their terriers with them and that these entered into the bloodlines of local strains. And it is undoubtedly this blood that helped improve greatly the loose, open coats that were so common among early Fell types; coats that meant they suffered in particularly harsh weather. The tight, harsh coat of the Irish terrier is the best type of jacket for resisting the elements and the fell-hunters of the Lake District have utilised this quality for generations. Fred Barker's famous terrier, Rock, certainly displayed this harsh, tight jacket and he worked some of the most hostile landscapes in the North of England for several seasons. It was Fred Barker's 'Chowt-faced' Rock, together with the two white and tan badger digging club terriers, which made up the foundation for what later became Anthony Barker's strain of terrier, though both Fred and Anthony were responsible for these bloodlines.

On the other side of the coin, the Barker strain, and the later strain bred by Sid Wilkinson, was descended from Jim Fleming's Myrtle; a terrier which saw much service with the Ullswater Foxhounds when Anthony Barker hunted the pack from 1941 until Joe Wear took up his post again when he returned from the war in 1946. Barker could have remained as Huntsman if he had chosen to do so, for his reign had been very successful through incredibly difficult years, but he was a shepherd and wished to get back to his duties full-time. Through the war years he had divided his attention 'twixt hunting hounds and farming the bleak fells around Patterdale. I have managed to trace the breeding of the terriers of Sid Wilkinson and Anthony Barker due entirely to the memory of Gary Middleton and Brian Plummer's superb book, *The Fell Terrier*. The exact breeding of every terrier is impossible to trace, for Fell terriers at that time were being bred in every village and almost on every farm and so one can imagine how easily names and bloodlines could be forgotten, but we have enough to help us see exactly why this strain of terrier has thrown out consistent workers for the last hundred years and more!

Each district and each hunt country was far more isolated during former times when transport was still rather primitive and so a good working terrier, dog or bitch, would be frequently used to produce offspring in that area, and sometimes beyond. Fred Barker's 'Chowt-faced' Rock stamped his type and ability into many families of earth dog and much of the blood found in the Ullswater country would have been descended from him. Anthony Barker's Rock was another much-used stud dog, but it was his son, Sid Wilkinson's Rock, that was to have the biggest ever impact on Fell and Lakeland terrier strains and his blood still runs strong today. But before delving more deeply into the history of this famous stud dog, let us first take a closer look at his breeding.

Fred and Anthony Barker had a dog from the old 'Chowt-faced' Rock/ badger digging club terrier strain and he had proven his worth working with the Ullswater Foxhounds over a number of seasons. He was tan and white in colour and was mated to Judy, the sister of Joe Wear's famous Tear 'Em, another outstanding worker who could kill foxes seemingly with little effort. Tear 'Em was bred out of Fleming's Myrtle, that same bitch which saw service with Anthony Barker at the Ullswater during the war years, and he had a massive head. As we will see, good, strong heads have become a trade mark of the Middleton strain and it was first Fred Barker's dog, Rock, and then the blood that produced quality terriers such as Tear 'Em, that was to put good head and bone into this strain.

Judy was a game bitch too and worked at the Ullswater, as have all of Fred and Anthony Barker's terriers, and this union produced, among others, a bitch that was given to Anthony's cousin. This bitch must have proven game, however, for Anthony brought her back into his breeding programme and had her mated to Jimmy Burcott's stud dog, though we have no recorded name for him. This mating produced Anthony Barker's famous Rock; one of the hardest and gamest terriers ever to come out of the Lakes country. Rock was then mated to Sid Wilkinson's bitch, Nettle, and this produced the wonderfully game and good-looking dog, Rock. Nettle was a well-bred bitch and sported quite a number of pedigree Lakeland terriers in her pedigree, but make no mistake, she was a wonderful worker and she served at the Ullswater for several seasons, proving a very good finder and bolter of foxes from the deepest of Lakeland borrans.

The strain that produced Nettle began when Joe Bowman gave Sid Wilkinson a white bitch named Lil. The Ullswater country had an influx of white-bodied terriers during Bowman's time as Huntsman and I believe this was due to the reputation gained by the terriers working at the Carlisle and District Otterhounds which hunted much of the same country as the Ullswater Foxhounds. In fact, when the otter and fox-hunting seasons overlapped, joint meets were sometimes held at local village pubs and the otterhounds would head for the river, while the foxhounds would head for the fells, so hunt staff knew each other well enough and the use of each others terriers would not have been an uncommon occurrence. Lil Foiler in particular, was a bitch who had proven incredibly game and she was bred out of Parson Russell's Fox terriers. She was also very good looking and produced many offspring that were both game and typey. Her influence on local Fell terrier strains was, I believe, tremendous and many of the white bodied terriers found in the Ullswater country long before Fred Barker imported his white badger digging club terriers, were, I am certain, descended from her.

Lil was mated by Crab, a terrier belonging to Braithwaite Wilson who had whipped-in to Joe Bowman and who had by this time taken over as Huntsman. Wilson hunted hounds from Bowman's retirement in 1924 until 1933 when Joe Wear took up the post, and he bred a very hardy strain of terrier of a type that had been used in the Patterdale area for decades, probably centuries; terriers that could stand up to the rigours of hunting some of the roughest and wildest terrain to be found in the British Isles, coping with extreme weather conditions admirably and being capable of killing reluctant foxes 'put in' by hounds. Wilson's strain was noted for its game and hardy qualities and Crab was one of his finest. From this union came Nettle.

This bitch proved such a good worker that Joe Wear took her with him to the Ullswater when he took up his post as Whipper-in, under the tuition of Braithwaite Wilson. It has to be remembered that breeders such as Sid Wilk's, and the Wilkinson family, Sid, his brother, and father Joe, were among *the* most important breeders the Lakes has ever produced, not only loaned their terriers out to local hunts, but they also did much private fox-hunting for farmers and gamekeepers. Sid's terriers saw quite a bit of service with the Ullswater Foxhounds, but they also saw much private work with Sid when

Fred Barker with terriers and badger dug using 'Chowt-faced' Rock. This trio of terriers founded the strain that was later continued by Gary Middleton.

Young Anthony Barker with Ilfracombe terriers and a hound from the Pennine pack at Ousby.

Diane Barker with a terrier descended from her father's, and grandfather's, strain.

Diane Barker's fell bitch, similar in type to Barker's Rock.

he dug foxes and badgers throughout the Ullswater country. A fell pack covers a large area and cannot control foxes in any one place too regularly, so terriermen of those days found much work for their earth dogs and many foxes were dug and either shot, or released out of sheep-rearing country. Sid Wilkinson enjoyed many private digs, but his terriers made a name for themselves working with the Ullswater pack in the main.

Nettle carved out quite a name for herself and was used quite extensively as a brood bitch. She produced some incredibly game and useful offspring and was such a good bitch that Joe Wilkinson based his strain of terrier on her. His bitch, also named Nettle, was bred down from Sid's'Nettle and she too proved extremely useful at work. Sid's Nettle then gave birth to Joe Wilkinson's Nettle and he took the bitch with him when he entered hunt service at the Ullswater when Joe Wear took over from Wilson as Huntsman. This gave the Wilkinson family plenty of opportunity to work their terriers with the hunt and they saw plenty of action in this capacity. Fell-hunters have always tested their terriers to the full, for the country itself is incredibly testing, and then breed off the gamest stock. Nettle proved very useful at work and she was put to Egdon Rock, one of the pedigree Lakeland terriers bred by Mrs Spence who often loaned her terriers to the Ullswater (those that didn't quite make the grade as show champions that is!), and this mating produced Joe Wilkinson's Rock.

The sire of Joe's Rock, Egdon Rock, must not be confused with today's pedigree Lakeland terriers. During those early days (1930s & 1940s in particular) the pedigree Lakeland still retained a very strong hunting instinct and the bad fights early breeders encountered were simply because the exhibits were bored with a show career and were frustrated because of not being allowed to exercise their desire for work. They still had good coats and often had very strong heads and jaws. They were narrow and easily spannable, without the exaggerated head length and depth of chest one sees today. And so many proved game and saw service at several of the fell packs, including the Ullswater, the Melbreak, the Eskdale and Ennerdale and the Blencathra. Indeed, it was such terriers that improved the looks of many strains of once rough and ready terriers and Hardasty's Turk and Wilk's Rock could only have been tidied up using such blood. Mrs Spence collected the most typey of all Fell terriers from throughout the Lakes country and these were the foundation for her kennel of pedigree Lakeland terrier that did so well during those early days, not only on the show field, but also at work with the foot packs of Cumbria. Egdon Rock had proven a worthy sire, for Joe Wilkinson's Rock also went into hunt service at the Ullswater and he proved game indeed.

My research has led me to discover that Anthony Barker did, in fact, have two well known terriers by the name of Rock; one a black and tan which saw service at the Ullswater when Anthony hunted hounds during the war, and a red dog which saw service at the same hunt a few years later. I am certain Anthony had other terriers of this name throughout his long and eventful life, but the two outstanding workers mentioned made such reputations that they are still talked about by the older generation of the Ullswater country. The red terrier, Rock, was Anthony's most famous and prolific worker and it was this terrier which sired Wilkinson's Rock, but the black and tan Rock was also a superb worker, though Anthony only ever referred to his red dog whenever 'Anthony Barker's Rock' was the topic of conversation.

It is my belief that the black and tan Rock was actually Joe Wilkinson's Rock, which had been sired by Egdon Rock. Joe whipped in at the Ullswater before the war and his terriers saw much service with this pack, hence it is not unreasonable to assume that Barker was loaned terriers during his time as Huntsman.

This mysterious black and tan Rock, which Eddie Pool say's was a large terrier who was extremely game and a hard fox killer, could, in my opinion, only have been Joe Wilkinson's Rock. If Anthony had owned any other famous terrier of this name, then surely he would have referred to it when interviewed by Plummer for *The Fell Terrier*! The fact that he failed to mention any other terrier, but the red dog, is, I am certain, proof that the black and tan Rock of the war years did not belong to him.

Eddie Pool hunted with this black and tan terrier on many occasions and he said Anthony worked him alongside a bitch named Whin, which was probably descended from Fred Barker's old strain. Eddie stated that Whin was a superb finder and a strong steady bayer who could bolt reluctant foxes. If foxes failed to bolt, or Anthony was hunting a lamb killing fox, then the Black and tan Rock was entered and the quarry dealt with below ground. Rock was a leggy, powerful terrier of a type Eddie Pool favours for hunting on the fells and he remembers this terrier far better than he does Anthony's red Rock. He does remember red Rock, however, and this was the terrier that was also given the name of 'Chowt-faced' Rock; the sire of Sid Wilkinson's Rock. Eddie tells a tale that illustrates just how game and useful Barker's Rock was. The Ullswater Foxhounds had been hunting a fox along the fellside overlooking Ullswater lake and they were now heading towards Brotherswater. The fox, being put under severe pressure by the pursuing pack, went to ground in a rock earth by the side of a steep ghyll and hounds were soon up, marking. Anthony was either not out that day, or he hadn't taken Rock with him, for the terrier had been left behind at the farm. However, he was loose around the yard and heard hounds as they hunted along the opposite fell. The Huntsman and Whip, together with a few of the more hardy and determined followers, eventually reached hounds and there they found that a terrier had already got to ground. They dug to the sounds of the raging battle and uncovered Barker's Rock, who had finished the fox after rushing to the spot from the farm across the valley. Eddie says that Barker's Rock was incredibly game and he accounted for many foxes in similar fashion. If a fox would not bolt, or could not, then very often a dig was unnecessary, for Barker's Rock was sure to finish the quarry. Where a fox lived, Rock would remain, until the job was done. Rock was so game, in fact, and had carved out such a fine reputation for himself, throughout the Lakes, not just around the Patterdale district, that tales told of his prowess, tales that could easily be verified by several witnesses, soon convinced Gary Middleton that this was the blood he wanted to use in order to 'spice-up' the Dent strain of terrier.

Joe Wilkinson's Rock was now put to a bitch sired by Arthur Irving's dog, Robin, and from this mating came Sid Wilkinson's Nettle II. Nettle was used with the Ullswater pack and privately, for digging both foxes and badgers, and she proved very game. Anthony Barker's Rock, now having the reputation as one of the best workers the Lakes has ever produced, was put to Nettle and from this inspired union came Sid Wilkinson's Rock – undoubtedly *the* most important Fell terrier stud dog of all time, for his progeny today are literally numbered in thousands.

Eddie Pool say's that Rock was incredibly hard and he should know, for he hunted with him on hundreds of occasions. Rock saw quite a bit of service with the Ullswater pack and was certain death to any fox that refused to make a bid for open ground. Apart from hunting with hounds, Eddie and Sid, along with a few others, would go out digging every Sunday and so Rock saw much work, though Eddie stated that Sid would protect Rock when it came to badgers, for the terrier was very hard and would surely come unstuck at this quarry, though Rock did work quite a number of badgers throughout his lifetime. Gary tells two interesting tales regarding badger digs with Rock and these illustrate just how game a terrier he was.

There is a badger sett close to the cottage where Sid lived when he worked for the Forestry Commission and a dig was organised at this sett. Gary dug every Sunday with Sid Wilkinson, Anthony Barker and very often Eddie Pool too, and on this particular day Gary's dog, Punch, was entered into the hole. It wasn't long before the terrier had found his quarry and then, once a little time had been allowed in order that the terrier and its quarry could settle in one spot, digging operations commenced. Punch stuck with his badger until, finally, the diggers broke through just behind the terrier. Sid would not enter Rock into deep setts, for the terrier would undoubtedly have come unstuck and Rock was as much a family pet as he was a working dog, hence his master was very careful about the type of earth and sett he would allow his beloved dog to work. If setts were shallow, Rock was entered, for the badger could soon be dug out, or sometimes Rock was used at the end of a dig, in order to draw the quarry, for he was a very powerful terrier.

At the end of this dig, Gary removed Punch so that Sid could give his terrier some work. Rock was loosed and he immediately flew into the tunnel, seized his quarry and drew it out. Badgers will often anchor themselves by digging their claws into the soil, so it takes a game and strong terrier to successfully draw such quarry from a tight hole-end. Rock drew many badgers in this manner throughout his long and prolific life. Rock, in fact, passed on this ability to draw badgers to many of his offspring and one of the hardest terriers of Rock's getting was a dog Gary named Mac. Mac could draw badgers from very bad places, even from under huge, immovable boulders, though sometimes he suffered badly, for he was so game that he would not back-off, no matter how severely his quarry retaliated. Sheila Barker told me about her times with this terrier, when her, Anthony and Gary would treat its wounds back at the Barker homestead after a Sunday dig. Sheila say's Gary was there every Sunday without fail and she would make them all a meal before they went off digging.

Sheila remembers one occasion when Gary, Anthony and a visitor from down south went digging and they returned with two badgers later that day. The badgers were taken alive and were being transported to the south where they would be released into an old, disused sett. She says that the two badgers were placed in sacks and put into the back of the car alongside two terriers. She cringed as she thought about that long journey and of the problems that would have been encountered on the way, with two terriers and two badgers sharing the same space! Sheila does not approve of Lakeland terriers being used on badger digs, for she say's they suffer very badly after being mauled by their quarry. She does have a point, for Lakeland terriers have been specifically bred to be hard and even the bitches, in many cases, will give little ground. Many are not fox killers, true, but they work their quarry hard and keep the pressure on throughout a dig. They have been bred thus in order to bolt reluctant foxes 'put in' by hounds. Dog terriers are required to kill foxes that will not, or cannot, bolt. When encountering badgers, they work them in the same manner and often come unstuck. Hence the reader may wonder why badgers were dug using Lakeland terriers by the older generation of fell-hunters during those times when it was legal, and often considered respectable, to do so.

Firstly, it was because badgers will take farm livestock, including lambs and poultry, and can make just as much a nuisance of themselves as can a fox, for a badger will return time and again in order to prey on vulnerable quarry such as chickens that cannot be got in at night. Indeed, Gary himself has lost many of his own chickens to badgers and he is certain of correct identification of the culprit, for he has seen their unmistakable prints in the snow. Hence many farmers and shepherds of the Lakes country required badgers to be moved from their land. Eddie Pool states that Glencoyne, in the Ullswater country, was the first place where badgers settled in this area, for he can remember a time when no badgers were found in the countryside surrounding Ullswater lake.

Secondly, badgers were dug simply because they are more readily found to ground, unlike foxes which spend much of their lives above ground, sleeping the daylight hours away in some chosen retreat free of the dust and gloom of an earth. Much of the south Lakes is made up of woodland and gorse coverts, so finding foxes below ground is not always easy. After a hard frost, or heavy snowfall, foxes will very often head below, in order to escape the severe cold, but at other times they can be difficult to find below ground, hence the reason why badgers were dug regularly by the older generation of fell-hunters. To give you some indication of how regularly Middleton dug badgers, we must turn to a diary he kept for a whole year, which records his hunting activities. Along with scores of foxes, he dug 137 badgers that year with a team of around 25 terriers and he states that, at times, he was short, for a few of these were youngsters unentered, or just starting. True, some of the harder terriers suffered, but many learned to tackle such formiddable quarry without receiving too much damage. Terriers such as Wilk's Rock, however, never learned to 'box clever' whilst engaging their quarry during a dig, and so harder earth dogs were either not used at all for such activities, or they were used as seizure dogs, or only entered into shallow setts, from where they could be dug out in a relatively short time. This meant that the damage was minimal to a terrier that lacked the sense to dodge attacks, rather than take them head on.

Gary told me of another dig with Wilk's Rock. He had travelled over to Glenridding and arrived at Sid's cottage in time to find him rather put out, for Rock, frustrated at a recent lapse in work, had killed one of his chickens. Rock's later years saw Sid's health begin to decline as he got older and so the terrier began to see less work than he was used to. Gary could see the badger sett up on the fellside not far from Sid's place and so he told 'Wilk's' that he would take Rock out for an hour or so. Gary climbed the fell and entered Rock into the sett, for he was eager to go and as keen as mustard for work. The terrier quickly found his quarry and Gary began to dig down to the furious soundings below, with Rock tackling his badger hard. Gary eventually broke through and took a badger from the sett, with Rock seizing and holding it at the end of the dig. Middleton then returned to Sid's cottage and Rock was by now a very different dog. As usual, he had refused to give ground and so had received a bit of a mauling. However, having exercised his strong working instinct, he was now once again more easily managed and he left the chickens alone!

The game qualities of Anthony Barker's Rock, and, more especially, the gameness of Sid Wilkinson's Rock, who also saw much service with the Ullswater foxhounds, as well as private Sunday digs with Eddie Pool, Anthony Barker and, later, Gary Middleton, convinced Middleton that this was indeed the strain that would 'spice up' his own Dent strain of working terrier; terriers which were game and quite hardy, but, as Gary stated, they would not 'die in a hole'. This may seem a rather callous statement to make, but it illustrates a point. A terrier that is willing to die in a hole is, in other words, one that will stay with its quarry and not give up until either dug out, or the quarry is bolted. Gary doesn't mean that he would literally leave a terrier to die in a hole, for he has taken part in some long and incredibly difficult digs in order to rescue a trapped terrier and has gone to great lengths to avoid losing any of his earth dogs which have found themselves in trouble. He just requires a standard of gameness that is simply faultless; one that sees the terrier in charge at all times, 'bossing' its quarry until dug out. This was not a new requirement. When one considers the terriers of the Highlands of Scotland, one comes across this same attitude that prevailed amongst the foxhunters of this wild and incredibly difficult terrain.

The ancestor of the modern Scottish breeds was an incredibly game terrier that, according to those who hunted foxes, badgers, otters and martens using the old Highland terrier strains, would stay in a hole until either the quarry, or the dog itself, died. Indeed, many reported having lost terriers to ground after they refused to leave their fox, which would not, or, more than likely, could not, bolt. The huge rock holes, known as cairns in Scotland, are impossible to dig and a terrier entering such a place is entirely on its own and must do its best to get out after killing, or bolting, its quarry. The same standard of gameness was, and still is, required of the terriers bred by Gary Middleton. The strain being produced by Sid Wilkinson and Anthony and Fred Barker, over in the Ullswater country, had produced a long succession of such game terriers and this impressed Middleton so much that he based his new strain entirely on Sid Wilkinson's Rock.

Not only did Wilk's Rock, and, indeed, other terriers from this line, including Nettle, his dam, have all of those qualities Middleton was seeking, but they also looked well too, doing very well at hunt and Agricultural shows throughout the Lake District and competing successfully with some of the best lookers the Lakes was producing at that time. True, working qualities were essential to Middleton, for he was incredibly busy at that time shifting foxes and badgers for farmers, shepherds and gamekeepers alike, but he also enjoyed the excitement of the showring and wished to produce terriers that looked as good as they worked. Hence the reason for taking his Dent strain bitches to Wilk's Rock and sons of Rock.

Gary knew Arthur Irving well at the time and he says that Art' was one of the best terriermen the Lakes has ever produced, rating him much higher than many fell-hunters such as those who have hunted fell packs and have built up excellent reputations as great houndsmen. Gary, in fact, believes few Huntsmen of fell packs make great terriermen simply because earth dogs are there to bolt foxes for hounds, or kill them below ground if they have proven troublesome, and few take them more seriously than this. He has a lot of respect for Johnny Richardson, for, he say's, Johnny took his terrier strain far more seriously, but he believes that the Irving brothers, Willie and Arthur, were, and still are, among the top terriermen of the county, even the country. And, Gary say's, for one reason; they knew how to produce both excellent workers and incredibly good-looking dogs too; something few other breeders can achieve. Many can produce excellent workers, while looks are rather lacking. Others can produce good-looking terriers, but working ability is lacking. Middleton, from very early on, had ambitions to emulate breeders such as Sid Wilkinson and Arthur and Willie Irving and his aims have always been to produce terriers that are pleasing to the eye, while at the same time are very useful to ground.

Willie Irving learned his trade under the guidance of Willie Porter of the Eskdale and Ennerdale Foxhounds, who bred a very hard strain of terrier, some coloured, some white, which were death to any fox which would not bolt. Irving became a passionate hound and terrier enthusiast and he began to breed a more classy strain than those found at Porter's kennels, though the foundation for his strain may well have come from Willie Porter who carried on the breeding programme of 'laal' Tommy Dobson. Irving then became professional Huntsman of the Melbreak Foxhounds and his strain of terrier became just as famous for its working ability, as for its looks. His terriers were certainly leggy and some show a decided hint of Bedlington terrier about them. Arthur Irving told Middleton that they emerged from an original blend of Bedlington, Fell and Fox terrier blood, though undoubtedly Irish terrier also played a part. Type was well and truly fixed in the Irish strains by the turn of the twentieth century and it is obvious to any who have a knowledge of dog breeds that such blood went into the mix that produced early Lakeland terrier types; photographs make that a certainty.

Many breeders at this time, although they were producing a rich red colouring on some, an obvious result of Irish terrier blood, were having problems with a rather grey grizzle, instead of the favoured black and tan colouring. Even the tan was grizzled and this poor and unattractive colour was due to Fox terrier blood being added to the mix. In fact, as Plummer states in *The Fell Terrier*, a great number of Lakeland terriers were white during the 1920s and 1930s; the period of time when Willie Irving was breeding top class workers and lookers. Willie preferred black and tans (though red terriers saw service at the Melbreak while he was Huntsman) and it is obvious that Welsh terrier blood was used in order to produce this rich black and tan, for that would be the only way in which Irving could have bred away from the poor whishy-washy colouring prevailing amongst Lakeland terrier strains at that time. As a result of his selective breeding programme, Irving succeeded in producing top quality terriers that could work three or four days a week with a fell pack and be good looking enough to win well at shows up and down the country. In fact, Irving's terriers were registered with the kennel club after recognition in 1921 and they won well at shows run by this organisation. They also greatly influenced the breeding of pedigree Lakeland terriers, though his dogs were far different to the modern pedigree dogs. They were leggy, narrow and easily spannable, but many

A sketch
of Sid Wilkinson with Rock

Trouble, an improved terrier from the Dent, Wilk's Rock strain.

Rusty, out of Toby and a top winning terrier.

were big and powerful enough to finish reluctant foxes in the deep borrans of his hunt country. Turk, a typey terrier he produced in the 1930s, was a renowned fox killer who saw many years of service with the Melbreak and greatly influenced both pedigree and unregistered Lakeland terriers. They were out and out workers, make no mistake about that, and Arthur Irving said that he had never seen one of Willie's terriers fail to make the grade as a top class worker. And no wonder, for Willie hunted during a golden age for fell-hunting and he had ample opportunity to provide plenty of work for quite a large number of his terriers.

In those days the Melbreak hunted a much larger country and they were not restricted by busy roads and mainline railways, as they are today. Irving, out of necessity, was required to cover all of his hunt country throughout the season and this was done by travelling to the more outlying country the day before hunting and staying in that area for the week. Hounds would hunt three or four days in an average week, usually starting on Tuesday and ending on Saturday, and then hounds would be taken back to kennels, or on to the next area to be blanket-covered.

Irving, along with his Whipper-in, like the other fell pack Huntsmen and Whips, could be away from home for up to two or three weeks at a time, while carrying out fox control throughout these different areas. There would be many followers during the Saturday meets, no doubt, and a wide choice of terriers would be available when a fox went to ground, but during the week far fewer people would be out, due to work commitments, and so the terriers belonging to Huntsman and Whipper-in would have plenty of work on for the two or three days hunted before the weekend set in. Willie Irving had several terriers and, as Arthur stated, they all went to fox. Like Willie, Arthur used the same strain of terrier when whipping-in at the Eskdale and Ennerdale, the Blencathra Foxhounds, and, later, when he returned as Huntsman of the Eskdale and Ennerdale Foxhounds. Even into old age, Arthur continued to use his typey strain of unregistered Lakeland terrier to fox, whenever he got the chance, and they proved game indeed, though one of his best was Robin, the grandsire of Nettle ll, which produced Wilk's Rock.

Gary continued breeding and working his Dent strain of terrier for a few years and he enjoyed much success as he ratted, dug and bolted foxes, and engaged regularly in badger digging with them. As already stated, this strain was game and very useful, but still, Middleton wanted something harder. Gary believes there was quite a bit of Bedlington blood in these terriers, but he also stated that they may have been bred out of some of Breay's old stock of working terrier, before he began breeding the Bull terrier influenced types now so well known. Josie Akerigg was a very keen fox-hunting man and Middleton states that he hunted around Dent, Sedbergh and Garsdale on a regular basis, following the Lunesdale pack, but also doing much private work for farmers and keepers, as did Buck and Breay. And so Gary is quite certain that his Great Uncle Dick used some of Akerigg's stuff to bring into his own strain. Cyril Breay would often give Akerigg terriers; rough haired tykes of no particular type, but resembling the rough and ready ancestors of breeds such as Yorkshire terriers. Lacking in looks, these were, however, incredibly game terriers and were used in the main for fox digging, bolting them to hounds, or waiting guns, as well as badger digs throughout North Yorkshire and Cumbria. But, although they proved game, Gary wanted something a little more special; a typey sort of terrier that would work its quarry hard and be capable of withstanding sub-zero temperatures in the midwinter.

In his later teens, he started attending many shows and regularly went to the Patterdale show where he met Sid Wilkinson and Anthony Barker. He had heard tales of the abilities of Barker's Rock and was very impressed with one particular terrier that Sid was exhibiting; his famous Rock whom Gary knew to have been sired by Barker's Rock; the red Rock, not the earlier black and tan dog which I am certain must have belonged to Joe Wilkinson, though this terrier was a grandsire of Wilk's Rock through Nettle ll. Gary knew the certainty of Rock's breeding and he soon came to see how game the dog was for himself. He stated that Rock would take severe maulings from badgers rather than give an inch (which is why Sid preferred not to use him unless the sett was shallow and Rock could quickly be dug out) and that he could kill foxes for fun, just like his sire. Indeed, Rock killed many foxes throughout his long life and any that refused to bolt would face certain death if this terrier was entered. He had superb bone structure too and, Gary say's, "he 'ad a 'ead like a brick." He was, in fact, just what Gary was looking for to improve the faults of the old Dent strain of terrier and so he resolved to use Rock, and sons of Rock, as much as he possibly could, in order to produce what he views as the true Lakeland terrier that was so popular throughout the Lakes at one time; a terrier that looked well, but that worked even better.

At that time most of the stuff being produced in the Ullswater country was bred out of three main stud dogs; Joe Wear's Tear 'Em, who was on loan from 'Ghillie' Fleming of Grasmere, Anthony Barker's red Rock and, a little later, Sid Wilkinson's Rock. As Gary stated, transport was far different then and so an outstanding working dog, or bitch, would be extensively used in each hunt country in order to produce good quality working stock. Rock had quite a bit of early pedigree Lakeland terrier blood in his veins, through the Egdon strain of terrier belonging to Mrs Spence and, of course, the dogs of Willie and Arthur Irving, which is why some of Middleton's stock shows a decided trace of pedigree Lakeland blood about it. Gary is often accused of using pedigree blood to improve the looks of his strain, but he is adamant that this is completely untrue. He would not use such blood to bring into his strain for two good reasons; the strain he has carried on and improved is far better looking than the pedigree Lakeland, and, more especially, is far more game.

Gary remembers many of Mrs Spence' pedigree Lakeland terriers and he states that Wilk's Rock was a far better looking dog than the best of the Egdon strain, including 'Lady of the Lake' which was a top winning terrier at Kennel Club shows. The Egdon stock were superb workers, however, but many were unused, especially the champions, and so the Wilkinson and Barker strains produced much more consistent stock. More especially, these terriers were more workmanlike than the pedigree stock and had far better jackets. Wilk's Rock had a coat like 'coconut matting', say's Gary, which, in my opinion, gives a strong indication that Irish terrier had played some part in the development of Lakeland terriers, both registered and unregistered strains, probably through the dogs of the Irving brothers and Mrs Spence. Roger Westmoreland can remember Irish terriers being brought to the Lakes many years ago by settlers and he stated that these entered into local Fell strains, so it is not unreasonable to suggest that Rock had quite a bit of this blood in his pedigree. In fact, Irish terriers of the eighteenth, nineteenth and early twentieth centuries were hard fox killing terriers and Fell terriers, both the untypey, and the good looking strains, worked in much the same manner. Whatever went into the mix, Wilk's Rock was a special sort of terrier and it was hard to fault him, though Gary say's that he was "just a little too big in the chest", if he was going to try to find fault with him.

Gary bred a litter out of Rock and one of his Dent strain bitches and then put the bitches out of that litter back to sons of Rock. From then on he used Rock himself, and sons of Rock, as much as he possibly could and continued to breed closely to this line. Rock was well known for stamping his type into his progeny and the first generation improved dramatically. Trixie was one of the first pups Gary bred out of Rock and she was very much his type. She was also a very hard bitch and a much-improved worker than the old Dent strain. Middleton worked her hard and, he say's, she worked like a dog, killing foxes quickly and allowing few to bolt. Like Rock, her sire, she "'ad a 'ead like a brick" and was generally of good conformation, with a superb jacket. Not only did this first generation work far better than the old Dent strain, immediately working more like traditional Lakelands should work, but they also looked far better too and Gary began doing well at shows from the first, for Rock did truly stamp his type into his progeny.

Middleton was so keen on improving his terrier strain that he took one of his bitches over to Sid Wilkinson's lakeside cottage during midwinter when it was snowing heavily. He had an old 125cc motorbike and he sat his bitch on the tank and began his perilous journey over the Kirkstone Pass, which was all but shut off to traffic. The snow was deep and Middleton never saw another car or motorbike on the roads as he sped on as best he could, unable to get out of first gear at any time during the journey and getting stuck once or twice on the way, but eventually making it to Sid's place. Wilk's stood there shaking his head at the madman who had set out on such a night, as Gary climbed off the motorbike looking like a snowman with his snowdog. The fact that he had risked his own neck meant nothing to the young Middleton, for, as he stated, "the bitch needed mating."

It wasn't the only time Gary would risk his neck over the Kirkstone Pass, for on several occasions during his younger, madder years, he rode over the pass on his motorcycle after a heavy session on the drink, when a day's hunting, or digging, would be celebrated in one of the local hostelries. It was at this time, when he was improving his terrier strain with as many additions of Rock's blood that he could muster, that he met Ruth, who remains his wife to the present day. They met in 1959 and were married in 1962 at Crook. They went on to have four daughters, Jackie, Barbara, Sue and Pauline and now have five grandchildren (at the time of writing).

Middleton, as well as digging foxes and badgers, also ratted quite regularly with his team of terriers, taking quite large hauls off the river Kent around Kendal, but doing particularly well at a tip not far from Crook which lies about half-way between Kendal and Windermere. Gary spent many a Sunday morning ratting at this tip and he says the face of the refuse dump was literally covered in rats and it looked as though the whole heap was moving there were that many. He could account for well over a hundred rats, and sometimes closer to two hundred, during a decent ratting session

Sid Wilkinson's Jenny, 1948, a grandam of Rock.

Crippin and Tim, vastly improved in type and working ability, out of Chip and Judy.

Trixie, out of Wilk's Rock and dam of old Rex.

Jewel, daughter of Trixie and Chip.

and he found the improved strain of working terrier well suited to such a task, for they were incredibly game and rat bite after rat bite didn't put them off in the slightest.

A Border terrier called Tim was often taken along by one of Middleton's friends, but it would not tackle a live rat. Once dead, however, Tim would go around collecting them up and piling his 'catch' in a heap. If any other terriers ventured too near, he would attack them, defending his little structure made up of dead rats taken by all the other terriers, but him.

One of his ratting partners was terrified of rats and always tied his sleeves and pant legs up with string, to prevent any fleeing rodent from using such places as sanctuary. Gary managed to tail a large buck rat and he quickly slipped it into this friend's pocket while he was distracted with the fast and furious action going on around him. Rats, once in a dark place, will settle quite comfortably, as they imagine they are safe. And so the large rat immediately settled down and the ratting went on at the usual pace.

On the way home, as was the usual custom after these ratting trips, the group stopped at the Brown Horse pub in the Winster valley, where a pint or two would quench a thirst that had been worked up for a good few hours. Middleton, knowing of the rat still hiding in that pocket, told his friend that it was his turn to get the fags out. He reached into his pocket and suddenly froze, the colour draining from his face far quicker than the beer was being drained from the glasses. Stuttering in utter fear, he managed to mumble that he had hold of a rat and asked what he should do next. Many folk had headed out into the country in order to enjoy Sunday lunch at a quiet country Inn, but they hadn't reckoned on Middleton's mischief! All of a sudden, and to the great surprise of the Landlord and his diners, the chap holding the rat suddenly screamed and, with flailing arms, threw the rat across the room. It landed on the carpet, ran across the lounge and then ran up the stairs, heading for the living quarters. Needless to say, the group of ratting enthusiasts were barred from their favourite 'on the way home' venue, for much of the foreseeable future.

Middleton, to say the least, was a rogue during his younger years and he felt a little hard done to by the actions of the Landlord, so, in revenge, he headed for the tip during the following Sunday and tailed six rats which he put into a shoe box. On the way home he stopped by the side of the country Inn full of Sunday lunch diners and tipped the rats out of the box and into the open window of the toilets which stands just above the road. It wasn't long before rumours were circulating of a rat infested public house in the

Winster Valley!!!

Ratting dogs need to be nimble, for one can be certain that these rodents will choose places where there are plenty of obstacles that will help them to escape. Rats can move at speed and they are incredibly agile, so a ratting terrier must possess the ability to dodge and weave through and around any obstacles in the way and it must be determined to reach its quarry and take it, if it is to be any good at the job. The improved strain of working Lakeland terrier, though much shorter coupled and box-shaped, proved very useful on rats and they were not only agile enough to cope with regular ratting sessions on local tips where obstacles were plentiful, but were also game enough to withstand severe bites, one after another, for hours at a time. In fact, these dogs thrive on such activities and the more bites they receive, the more determined they become in seeking out these disease-ridden pests. And so the more typey, more hardy and much harder strain Middleton was now breeding, became a much better all-round worker, as well as a much better looking terrier.

Eddie Pool stated that many fox killing terriers do not make good finders and he quoted a few examples of terriers that have seen service with the Ullswater pack. In these instances, a baying sort of terrier would be put to ground first and then, if the fox refused to bolt, the harder terrier would be entered. Finding ability will be the subject for our next chapter.

A working Lakeland, Tim.

Rags, the son of old Rex, and Jed, the near-black terrier, who served at
the North Lonsdale Foxhounds and was used to finish reluctant foxes.

Tim and Jed with Jack, a good foxing lurcher.

A dig at Kirkby Lonsdale. L-R: John Bell, Jackie Robinson, Gary Middleton,
Jakey Howard and Arthur Wells.

Hoot.

Nettle, a veteran at eight years (Gary dug five badgers in one day using this bitch).

Candy.

Spike, out of Wilk's Jock. He entered on his first dig when Gary took two badgers with him.

Tim, out of Rock (one of the terriers returned to Sid Wilk's and passed on to Gary).

Rusty, loaned to keeper who sent it to Bramham Moor Hunt.

Rex, son of old Rex. This terrier has a head similar to Fred Barker's Rock.

Rex, Nettle and Punch. Punch worked with hill pack in Wales.

Chapter Two

GOOD FINDERS?

Nose must be rated as the highest priority in a hunt terrier in the Lake District, and for good reason. The borrans and crag earths of this area are often incredibly vast and a terrier to ground in such places must have the ability of finding its foe, wherever it may be. Foxes can move around borrans as an earth dog searches and one can imagine how confusing it can be for a terrier working a mass of different tunnels which are full of fresh scent. Working out exactly where a fox lies must be incredibly difficult and only the best can hope to succeed in such circumstances. Eddie Pool say's that many hard fox killing terriers are lacking in nose and that baying types are used to find a fox, in the hopes that it will bolt, and then harder terriers are entered afterwards, in order to finish the fox below ground should it refuse to budge; a traditional method of controlling fox numbers in this part of the world.

It is my belief that, because harder terriers are often used in this way, as a sort of last resort, they do not really develop the art of finding, simply because they are often not given the opportunity. I am certain that many of these harder terriers would find just as effectively as any other terrier, if used for locating the fox in the first place. The only trouble with this system is, that few foxes would be capable of bolting once a harder terrier was up to them. Terriers such as Joe Wear's Tear 'Em and Anthony Barker's Rock allowed few foxes to bolt.

Having said this, there are going to be some terriers that lack nose and Eddie mentions a bitch he had, Peggy, which was a daughter of Wear's Tear 'Em and, although she was an excellent worker, he said that she was lacking a little in nose, which basically means that she must have struggled a little in larger borrans that are so vast they have to be seen to be believed. I question this though, for where one terrier is put into a massive earth with tunnels all over the place, the fox will give it the run around all day and so a terrier could end up emerging after a time, seemingly having failed to find, but in reality being unable to pin down its fox because of the sheer size of the earth. Very often more than one terrier will be entered into such a massive rockpile, in order to prevent the fox from keeping ahead of its foe. Terriers that fail to find, even in smaller earths, I believe, in 99 cases out of 100, do so simply because they are cowards. Of course, there are exceptions and sometimes it is true that a hard fox killer will lack when it comes to finding ability. Indeed, Gary himself has owned such a terrier. A bitch would be used to locate the fox and then the hard terrier was entered. It would then go to its quarry and kill it quickly and with little fuss, but it would not seek out foxes by itself. Maybe something happened during its early entering that can account for this strange habit. It is possible, I suppose, that, if a youngster is entered towards the end of a dig when a more experienced terrier has done much of the work, that the baying of that dog imprints on the mind of the puppy and, rather than being unable to find, simply needs to hear another terrier at work, before it will seek out its quarry. Maybe a therapist could help explain such things!

The young Gary Middleton, now having started to improve his terrier strain, put finding ability at the top of his list, for he is a traditionalist and believes that a terrier must have good nose if it is to be an effective tool against fox predation. Middleton was a keen badger digging man and hunted foxes with equal enthusiasm, so would the new strain live up to his high expectations?

Middleton took a trip over to Ireland, a place where he has done much fox-hunting and badger digging over the years, and he was entering a black and tan bitch named Judy. She had never even seen a hole before, let alone worked quarry, and so Middleton had no idea of how things would turn out. A fell/Lakeland, known as a border/Lakeland, was entered and it emerged a little while later, showing no further interest in the earth. However, Judy, at fifteen months of age, was showing interest and pulling at her lead, and so Gary Loosed her, glad that she could have a bit of experience at working below ground, even if the earth was empty.

He loosed her and she disappeared below ground as though she was a veteran at this game. He expected her to run the empty earth and emerge soon afterwards, but a few minutes later she had not returned, and so they began searching. This was in the days before locators and the old fashioned method of 'ear to the ground' was used. They found her half an hour later, baying at a spot fifty yards up the field. The earth was much bigger than they had first thought and the border/Lakeland was either a poor finder, or it just wasn't interested in the quarry below ground.

Thankfully, the earth wasn't too deep and digging operations began. They broke through to the young, inexperienced bitch within quite a short time and she had bottled up two large badgers, which, as you can imagine, were giving her quite a rough time of it. The earth itself was too large to be entering a novice there and the quarry more than a little testing, yet Judy had taken it in her stride and had proven both a good finder, and a game worker. Judy was a daughter of Rock, a game terrier that was given to Middleton, along with its brother, Tim, after the pair had been returned to Sid Wilk's because they were destructive and unmanageable. The pair had been kept as pets and were bred out of a son of Rock and Johnny Richardson's Titch, a leggy black and tan bitch which was a wonderfully game terrier to fox and saw much service with the Blencathra Foxhounds. Both Rock and Tim, once entered, became extremely useful terriers and Tim was sold to a chap at Bladen where he saw much work.

Judy had made a promising start to her career and she went on to become an incredible worker, one that, like a traditional dog Lakeland, could finish foxes that would not bolt. Gary tells a curious tale of a 'hunt' with Judy that displayed just how game some of these terriers can be. One of the fell packs were experiencing a severe shortage of foxes in a particular area of their hunt country and they approached Gary and asked if he could provide them with live foxes that would help replenish stocks. Exactly why there was such a shortage Middleton cannot say, but my guess is that someone was over-shooting in that area, or there had been an outbreak of disease such as distemper, which had all but wiped out the vulpine race in that district. The fact that other foxes were not moving into the void left by this decrease in numbers also say's much about the population round about, which also must have been low (thus giving some credence to the theory of an outbreak of distemper). Anyway, Middleton had a reputation for being able to procure foxes and he gladly obliged.

It must be stressed that this was not done in order to hunt these foxes, but so that the released vulpines would breed and re-stock the area. This was many years ago too and such actions were not frowned upon as they are now, for this was a different era to today, when political correctness has gone mad! And so Gary had no qualms about obliging the hunt and quickly set about the task. Using nets to capture foxes bolted by his terriers, and by digging many too, he eventually had 30 foxes settled in a large shed close to the Sun Inn at Crook, which were destined for life in a different part of the country.

The Huntsman and one of the hunt committee arrived shortly afterwards and Gary took them to where he had stored the foxes. Upon opening the door, however, he discovered that all 30 had escaped through a small hole they had dug in the wooden floor, which must have started rotting in places. Zinc panels covered the gap underneath the shed, but a small hole allowed him to shine a torch into this pitch-black space. Hardly believing his eyes, he saw all thirty of them crouched in the darkness, obviously awaiting the coming of nightfall when they would have made for the open fields and rock-strewn fells – and freedom! This was a problem, for they knew not how to get them out of there without killing, or badly injuring, them, for Gary would have been strung up by the local shepherds had he allowed all thirty foxes to escape into the surrounding countryside which was 100% sheep-farming country. Middleton, however, being a resourceful sort of chap, thought of a way that might just work.

He had Judy in the van and went to fetch her, without saying a word to his companions. He collected a length of rope and tied it to his terrier's collar, before releasing her into the darkness below the shed, through the small gap in the zinc panels. She was by now an experienced bitch and had proven hard at working both fox and badger. She was also a typey bitch and Middleton had done well with her at shows throughout the Lakes country. She entered like a wildcat and latched onto the nearest fox. Gary then drew her out, knowing she would not let go, and fox number one was easily secured and put into a sack. This carried on for quite some time until, at long last, all thirty foxes had been drawn out from under that shed and all were secured in sacks in readiness of release into new country. The project worked and shortly afterwards the once depleted area was holding a decent number of foxes again. Before he left with his haul, the Huntsman turned to Gary and asked how much he wanted for his terrier bitch, he was that impressed by her game qualities, for she had received several bites during the whole operation and hadn't flinched in the slightest – qualities undoubtedly inherited from the bloodlines of the Barker and Wilkinson strains.

Anyone who is shocked by such tactics should first of all know that using terriers in this manner was once common practise in the Lake District. Some rock earths, although undiggable because of huge granite slabs sinking into the very depths of the earth, are really quite shallow and may only be a few feet out of reach of the Huntsman. Alternatively, an earth may have been dug, possibly for several hours, and, only a few feet from completion, the diggers hit huge boulders several tons in weight that simply cannot be shifted. In such cases, fell-hunters often resort to tying a rope to a harder terrier and then entering it to the quarry, which is skulking just out of reach.

The hard terrier then latches onto its fox and will not usually let go, unless it be to get a better purchase, and the terrierman then pulls on the rope, slowly, slowly, until, at last, the fox is pulled out of the tunnel and is secured. Remember, hunting in places such as the English Lake District is not about sport, but about controlling fox numbers. A great many of the followers and supporters, indeed, even hunt staff, are made up of shepherds and so controlling a common agricultural pest is the first and foremost priority. And so these hunters of this bleak and hard landscape will go to great lengths in order to catch their prey and this determination and sheer grit has produced hounds and terriers of outstanding abilities in the face of great odds.

Anthony Barker sometimes resorted to this method of drawing a fox out of a tight spot where it was skulking just out of reach and this say's something about the game qualities his earth dogs possessed. Hounds had put a fox to ground at a rock spot in Mardale and Barker was soon up with his terriers. He entered Tinker and she latched onto her quarry and Anthony was then able to slowly draw out a large dog fox that had been taking lambs in some of the wildest country hunted by the Ullswater pack, or any other pack for that matter. Of course, this method was never used if the fox was any deeper than just a few feet out of reach. In many cases, it is the only way of getting a fox out of an earth that is utterly impossible to dig.

Earths of this type do not exactly test finding ability, but for every one shallow refuge such as those described, there are a score of deep borrans that are so vast many are not even worked anymore, for they prove impossible places from where to bolt foxes. Such earths do test finding ability and it is no wonder that the fell-hunters have developed a working terrier that can find foxes anywhere. Very often there are ledges in such earths too and foxes can get out of reach of even hard terriers, so attempting to work these places is usually a futile operation. I know of such places myself and no longer work them. One such place is a vast borran below a long line of crags high up in the Western Pennines. This is a bleak place and takes the full force of the winter weather coming off the icy depths of the tempestuous Irish Sea, so a terrier working in this region must be hardy and have a good dense jacket that will ward off the wet and cold. Many of the earths are in cold rock too, so a terrier to ground must be capable of coping with freezing temperatures and anything else the midwinter throws at them.

I was once out with hounds in this valley and a fox was marked to ground. Fell was put in and Mist soon joined him, for, although fully capable of dealing with a fox on his own, it was under some huge boulders and he couldn't find a way through, so another terrier may just have speeded up the process. After a good forty-five minutes or so of trying desperately to get to their foe, with myself attempting to open up other places by removing the smaller rocks as best I could, I had to give it up as a bad job in the end, for that fox knew it was secure and wasn't going to budge in the slightest. The very next season another fox was marked to ground in this same place and yet again the terriers could not find a way through, no matter how hard we tried to get them on. They went wild with frustration as the hot scent wafted through the mass of piled up rocks and they scrambled all over the place, searching, searching for a way through, but still, they could not quite reach their foe which had got itself into an incredibly tight spot. In a soil earth, a terrier can dig on, if it has the heart to want to reach its quarry, but in rock it is impossible for a terrier to get into tight spaces, no matter how hard they try. I simply avoid this earth nowadays, knowing it is futile to even attempt working it. The Lake District has many such earths where foxes head for sanctuary when hard-pressed by hounds.

Finding ability in the new strain of working Lakeland Middleton was now breeding, when one considers their history, was as one would imagine it to be – second to none. Gary worked his terriers in a wide range of earths, from dug-out rabbit holes, to deep borrans, to huge badger setts, and that all-important ability was there. One of these early terriers was Jock and he had entered exceptionally well at his first ever dig (see chapter three). A day out in the north-east of England was to display just how good this new strain was at finding.

Middleton had been up that way for a show and he was invited out on a dig, but had little hope of using Jock, as there were several other terriers there that were more likely to be used. They walked to quite a large earth mainly dug around massive tree roots and, sure enough, one of the terriers belonging to a local lad was tried first. There were seven other terriers there besides Jock and all seven were entered before Jock got his chance. Some said that there was nothing in, disappearing into the darkness of the musty tunnels, having a route around and then emerging soon after, showing little, if any, interest, while others were quite keen, but they too returned after a short time to ground, interested, but seemingly unable to reach their quarry. Middleton was certain something was at home, either a fox, or a badger, and at last Jock was given an opportunity.

Jock entered quickly and was soon telling his master that there was indeed some form of quarry at home, but, like some of the others, he was seemingly unable to get up to his foe. However, unlike some of the others who had given up after a time and had returned, Jock carried on digging and eventually managed to make a way through. He settled in one spot soon afterwards and then Gary and his companions began digging. It was a difficult place and two hours later they broke through to where Jock had managed to bottle up a single badger. 'Brock' must have been digging on as the other terriers were tried and it must have settled in a chamber, where Jock eventually managed to dig on to it. Finding ability in such difficult conditions is essential and Jock had displayed superior finding ability, as well as determination to reach his quarry.

It was this same Jock which sired Nailer, when mated to either Nettle, or Trixie (Middleton cannot remember exactly who was his dam); an ultra-game Lakeland terrier that would face fox or badger with exactly the same intent; to kill, or be killed. Nailer was exceptionally hard and didn't flinch while at work, not giving an inch, no matter how severe a drubbing he received. At this time, when Nailer was in his prime, George Newcombe was looking for outcross blood for his Rillington strain of Bedlington terrier, which, he said, was getting a little weak and was in need of fresh blood, and so he chose Nailer as a stud for one of his bitches, impressed by how game this dog was. An acquaintance of Middleton's recently reminded him of this mating, for he has Bedlingtons that are descended from this very outcross programme and, Gary assures me, they are excellent workers. Newcombe sometimes bred Bedlingtons that were a little on the large side and he would dig quarry with his Lakelands and then use these larger terriers as seizure dogs. Of course, a good many were small enough for earthwork, especially after this mating with Nailer, and they proved game indeed; finding, staying, or killing those that would not bolt. In fact, Newcombe's Bedlington terriers served with a number of different packs of hounds and they served these hunts well.

Rock, of Sid Wilkinson's kennels at Glenridding, sired numerous litters of puppies and at one time the Ullswater country was full of his progeny, so Middleton had several options open to him, using Rock, sons of Rock and Grandsons of Rock in order to capture as much of that blood as he possibly could. This, in time, meant that he locked in those qualities that had made the Barker and Wilkinson working terrier strains so well known and this resulted in producing more consistent numbers of excellent workers and top winning terriers. The hunt with the Lunesdale foxhounds and the subsequent dig with Chip, one of the early terriers from Rock's getting, illustrates just how useful this strain of terrier was. After the two fell terriers had emerged, uninterested in the further proceedings, Chip was entered and soon found his quarry, when a battle royal took place. Gary dug hard, having to squeeze into tight spaces where he managed, with time and more than a little effort, to pull rocks out, one after another. He eventually uncovered his terrier and there he discovered a hole going off to the left and another going off to the right, with a badger in each side. Chip was having to tackle the pair of them, yet he never flinched, but stuck to his task with grim determination. The fox had perished behind them and Chip was undoubtedly keen to get to it, but other distractions prevented him from doing so! What game terriers were being bred from this mix of Dent strain terriers and Wilkinson's famous Rock.

One of the gamest terriers ever to be bred in the Lake District was to come out of this mix and in 1969, or thereabouts, Middleton bred a puppy that was to become the hardest, gamest earth dog Gary has ever seen. He was a black and tan dog and Middleton named him Rex, which is a name he has given to many terriers over the years, so the unravelling of pedigrees is very difficult. However, this Rex is unmistakable, for he not only won the Great Yorkshire show, but he was also a far harder terrier than any Gary has ever bred, either before his coming, or afterwards, even all these years later.

Rex had a massive head and, like Wilk's Rock, would quickly finish any fox that refused to bolt. In fact, Rex gave foxes few chances of bolting. If they did not move and get out of an earth before Rex reached it, then a fox was sure to die, for Rex would not bay and Gary never heard him bark once while to ground, not even when working 'Brock'. He learned to dig to bumps and furious grunts as his terrier took hold of its quarry and demolished it.

Exactly how Rex was bred is difficult to say, for Middleton has bred that many terriers that he has lost track of several bloodlines and simply cannot remember. However, this was in the early days, so he was probably a grandson of Wilk's famous Rock. He was bred out of Rock, that is for sure, as are all of Middleton's terriers, but how many lines he carried back to this dog I do not know, though I suspect it was several. In fact, Middleton bred incredibly closely to Rock's bloodlines and has succeeded in capturing and locking in all of those qualities that had made the Barker and Wilkinson strains so popular. Gary thinks that the dam was a bitch called Tiny, which was one of the early improved types and she was probably a daughter of Rock, or maybe a daughter of a son of Rock, for Gary used quite a few at that time and he mentions one or two. A terrier named Rex was bought from Sid Wilkinson by a chap at Staveley and Middleton says that this was a very game dog, which he used quite a bit on his bitches. So Tiny may well have been out of this dog, or another of Rock's sons. He thinks the sire may have been a dog named Tim and this, he is certain, was a son of Rock himself. The other possibility is that Chip, the terrier featured in the introduction, was the sire of Rex, though he thinks that a son of Rock owned by a chap at Hartsopp Hall was the sire of this dog, which would make Rex a great grandson of Rock, if Chip was the sire. However, it was one of these two terriers that sired Rex and something went into this dog that made him just that bit more special than most other terriers.

True, Middleton's strain was already producing a large number of fox killing types, even some of the bitches, but Rex was different. I myself have owned hard terriers that could kill foxes, but usually Reynard has a chance at bolting, even when a harder terrier has been working it for a while. The combatants separate for just a few seconds and the fox turns and is gone. With Rex, though, there was no cautious approach, no baying, nipping and teasing until the dog could outwit its quarry and move in for the kill. No, there was none of that. Rex simply charged into an earth and grabbed his fox as soon as he reached it. From then on, he simply destroyed his quarry very quickly; crushing it with his massive head and powerful jaws in no time at all. A keen foxhunter once dug to this terrier and all he had to go on were bumps somewhere underground. He uncovered his first fox, which was dead, but the terrier was gone. More bumping and he then dug some more and uncovered a second fox, dead, but, again, with no sign of Rex. He followed yet more sounds of bumping and uncovered Rex just finishing off his third fox.

George Norman, a chap who lives in West Cumbria and who has some superb fox catching lurchers, remembers Rex well and once saw him at work. He was out in the hills in the Scottish borders when he came across Gary Middleton and Jimmy Monteith of Glasgow, engaged in a dig up in the hills, on a steep hillside. Rex was to ground and Middleton said that Rex had killed one fox and was now in the process of killing another. George was a little sceptical, however, but awaited the outcome. Middleton and Monteith dug down to Rex and they uncovered him as he was just finishing his second fox. Gary said there was another dead one in there and so a baying bitch was put in and she soon started barking. They dug to her quite quickly and there they uncovered another dead fox. Gary knew that Rex would not leave a fox alive in an earth if it didn't bolt and get out of there very quickly.

Rex was not only a very hard fox killer and a dog that had destroyed livestock killing foxes for the Lunesdale hunt (Middleton hunted quite a bit with the Lunesdale in those days), but he had also proven a very good finder too. Many older fell-hunters say that a good fox killer rarely makes a good finder too, but Gary disputes this. He has produced many terriers that were both great finders, as well as fox killers, and the fact that his earth dogs have served with several hunts, including the Lunesdale, North Lonsdale, Coniston and Bramham Moor hunts, tells the reader something of the abilities of this strain. The fact that Gary has produced great finders in both his dogs and his bitches, may be due to his allowing them to develop as such, rather than just using harder terriers after others have failed to bolt their fox, which is how the fell packs operate and possibly why many of their fox killers are not considered as good finders! All a harder terrier has to do, once the bitch is called out, is to follow the scent of its companion straight to the fox. On many occasions, however, harder terriers do not enjoy even this amount of work, but are simply put in at the end of the dig in order to draw out the fox from a tight spot. As you can imagine, finding ability has no chance to develop when such methods are employed.

I have just received a telephone call from Gary Middleton that has at last cleared up the mystery of the breeding of 'old Rex', as Gary calls him. The Rex bred out of Tiny and either Chip, or Tim, was another dog and Middleton is easily mixed up simply because he uses more or less the same names with each successive generation. With time and effort, Gary has managed to trace the breeding of Rex and he is certain that his mother was a red bitch named Trixie, the one with "a 'ead like a brick'. She was put back to Wilk's Rock, breeding as closely to the line as Gary dared, and this mating produced the gamest and hardest terrier Middleton has ever seen – Rex. And this breeding makes much sense, for Middleton had bred as closely to Rock's line as he possibly could and those game qualities came out in this dog to an extreme degree as a result. I confess I almost deleted what I had already written about the breeding of this dog, after this phone call, but I have decided to leave it in the book in order to show the reader exactly how complicated the unravelling of pedigrees and bloodlines can be, especially when the strain goes back fifty years and more!

Both Rock and Trixie had very large, powerful heads and this resulted in Rex having one of the most magnificent heads found on any Lakeland terrier. His head, coupled with his courage of course, meant that he could kill foxes almost casually and sometimes without receiving a single bite. Badgers were completely dominated by him and, on a few occasions, he even killed fully-grown badgers. I know this is very difficult to believe and Middleton was wary of telling me this, because he knows many will think him a liar, but this has been confirmed by Barry Wild who actually dug to Rex on several occasions when Gary had loaned him to Dave Roberts of Manchester. Barry has uncovered badgers that had been throttled by Rex on one or two occasions, which backs up what Middleton had told me.

Rex was put into quite a shallow sett (like Sid Wilkinson, Gary would not put his harder dogs too deep in badger setts, lest they got into trouble) and the usual bumps and grunts began. Middleton dug down to his dog and he there uncovered the terrier and a dead fully-grown badger. There were hardly any marks on it, so he presumed it had suffered heart failure. However, at another dig, he uncovered his terrier again and this time he was in no doubts at all that Rex had killed the badger, for both dog and quarry were in a mess. When the same thing happened a third time, Middleton was convinced that Rex could, in a few cases, kill 'Brock'. This is difficult to accept, I know, but I suppose it is possible if a dog finds a way of getting to a badger's throat and then throttles it. Certainly, if a terrier, no matter how big the head, how powerful the jaws, went jaw to jaw with 'Brock', it would come unstuck every time and the only way any terrier could hope to succeed is somehow to develop a knack of getting to the throat and closing off the windpipe. Barry Wild has uncovered badgers that Rex has throttled, so obviously this was indeed the case. Maybe the powerful head and jaws helped him to accomplish this. In most cases, however, Rex did not manage such a feat, but Middleton says that those he dug out using this dog would not face him and were doing their utmost to get away from him. He has never before, or since, seen a terrier that could 'boss' a badger in such a way.

Rex, as we have seen, was a son of Wilkinson's Rock and inherited those game qualities to an extreme degree. This mating completely undermines yet another theory that was, and still is, common in livestock breeding circles; that elderly studs do not produce very good offspring. Rex was bred in 1969, or thereabouts, which means that Rock was getting on a bit by this time, yet Rex was the strongest and gamest dog Middleton has ever produced. Rock, in fact, remained at stud right into old age and he sired legions of incredibly good looking and working terriers. One of his progeny in his later years was Jock; a typey black and tan dog which had a white blaze on its chest. Wilkinson's Jock was very game and, like his sire, was a hard fox killer. Middleton is pretty certain that Dave Roberts' famous dog, Rip, was out of Wilk's Jock, or possibly Hector, another game dog from Wilkinson's breeding. Rip was incredibly game and many working Fell and Patterdale terriers are descended from him. But back to Middleton's Rex, which sired Rags.

Middleton was at a show in the Lakes and a farmer was boasting in the beer tent about the abilities of his dog, Basher. When terriermen get together at shows and the beer glasses begin emptying, the talk often turns to who has the best dog. This farmer was adamant that his dog was better than any to be found anywhere and so Gary, being young and up for a challenge, stepped in and dared to say that he might have a dog that could show Basher a thing or two. The farmer immediately responded by inviting Middleton up to his farm for a badger dig and Gary eagerly accepted, taking Rags with him to the farm, which, Gary told me, was somewhere near Coniston.

Basher was put into a drain and he there found a badger skulking in the darkness of the pipe. The end of the drain narrowed to a very small drainage pipe and so there was only one way in and out. Basher was certainly game and Middleton stated that the dog was a grand worker, if one wanted a baying sort of a dog. But this challenge was about who had the gamest terrier and Rags was about to have his chance, once the farmer had managed to get his dog out of the hole. Rags entered very eagerly, took hold of his quarry immediately and, within two minutes, had drawn 'Brock' from out of that pipe and the whole thing was over and done with. Middleton won the three pound wager (which was quite a sum in those days) and went home the winner.

On another occasion Gary had won a show with Rex and afterwards had a bit of a walk out with a few of the North-eastern terrier lads. A badger was located behind some bales in a barn and eight terriers were tried. Only one showed interest in the proceedings, but it was discovered that this was baying two-feet away from its quarry. Again, Rex was loosed and within minutes he had drawn his quarry out from its hiding place. And experiences like this can be multiplied a hundred-fold, for the number of foxes and badgers Gary dug with this dog are too numerous to mention. In fact, Middleton did that much work with Rex that he cannot remember most of them, just those that were a little out of the ordinary. Like a dig in Ireland that began in a rather unpromising fashion. Middleton took Rex and his son, Jock, with him to the emerald Isle and two fell-type terriers were also out that day. One of the fells was put in and it explored the earth, before returning soon afterwards. The second fell terrier went in and looked around for a while, before it too emerged, saying nothing was at home. Jock was inexperienced at this time and so Gary said he would loose him and allow him to have a look through the earth "seein' as there were nowt in".

Jock went in and was gone for quite some time and then, shortly afterwards, a badger bolted. Rex was pegged down a little way from the earth and he caught the badger as it ran past and held onto it. Jock then settled in one spot and a seven-foot dig followed, which took all afternoon to accomplish, before the terrier and the two badgers he had bottled up, could be reached. The owner of the two fell terriers must have been very disappointed, but to be fair to him many Fell terriers will not work badgers, even though they are incredibly good fox dogs, as these two undoubtedly were.

This is because, in the main, Fell terriers have been discouraged from working such quarry. True, many did dig badgers using this breed before this testing activity became illegal, but a significant number were strictly fox-hunting folk who did not want their terriers badly mauled, and thus put out of action for two, three, even four, weeks at a time. And so, over time, many strains produced offspring that were simply not inclined to look at badger, even though they were as keen as mustard to go to foxes. Eddie Pool has bred a number of terriers that would not even look at a badger and one of these was Wasp. In her latter years, however, as her career was coming to an end, she suddenly decided that badgers were fair game and entered to them like a wildcat.

Since the ban, of course, Fell terriers have been discouraged from entering to such quarry (badgers are encountered in fox earths, even rockpiles, on occasion and one can only discourage one's terrier from working them) and thus there may now be even larger numbers that will simply show little, if any, interest in badgers if they are found skulking inside what is obviously a fox earth. It is illegal to enter a terrier into a badger sett and the signs of occupancy are obvious, such as large mounds of soil, or sand, outside the den. Large, well used entrances and worn pathways leading to and from the sett. Fox earths have none of those signs and so one cannot possibly know if a badger has popped into such an earth for the day, maybe having been driven out of its usual abode by an aggressive boar, or it may have been disturbed and simply entered the nearest refuge. In such cases, it is very handy to have a terrier that will not work badgers. But in Middleton's case, during those long lost days when badger digging was legal, he required all of his terriers to work them and any that would not, were usually sold to fox-hunting enthusiasts, or simply sold as show dogs. Gary requires all of his terriers to work hard and in those days, when he was in his prime, his schedule was very punishing indeed and his terriers were tested to the utmost. Now, of course, with badger digging illegal and terrier work to fox severely limited in England and Wales, it is difficult to test terriers to the utmost, though the Middleton strain on the whole, make no mistake, still make excellent working terriers.

Middleton tells a tale about Rex that also demonstrates just how game a dog he was. Gary stated that, when Rex was put to bitches, he had to be careful for, if the bitch got aggressive, particularly when they tied, he was liable to snap and attack it, such was his bad temper. On one occasion, at a show, a chap was stood at the ringside and he was full of tattoos, complete with vest and a harness strapped to a thickset Staffordshire Bull terrier that was barking and growling at all the exhibits, showing all the signs that it wanted to be free in order to kill every other dog in sight. The Lakeland dog class came round and Middleton was entering the ring with Rex. As he bent down to go under the rope, the lead loosened a little and Rex had enough rope to reach the Bull terrier. As powerful as it was, Rex had it turned over on its back and was worrying it, long before it realised what was going on. The dog turned out to be a coward, for it screamed in fear and tried to get away from the antagonist. Middleton got his dog off and the chap slunk away, his image (not to mention his ego) now completely deflated! Brian Nuttall believes that Fell terriers are gamer dogs than even Bull terriers and in this particular case that proved to be true.

Gary tells another tale of a Staffordshire Bull terrier and two Welsh lads who invited Middleton and his digging partner down for a spot of Badger hunting. They arrived at a sett and Middleton put one of his terriers in. It wasn't long before it had settled in one spot and the digging began. They eventually had quite a deep trench dug and finally broke through to terrier and badger. Middleton was clearing a space and managed to get his dog out of the way in readiness of tailing the quarry, when an iron bar shot past the side of his head and went straight through the unfortunate badger. While it was struggling against death, the Bull terrier was loosed and it began worrying the poor beast. The dog was battle-scarred, so was probably used in such ways fairly regularly. However, such cruelty sickened Middleton and his partner and they turned on the two Welsh lads and gave them a hiding, telling them never to get in touch again. Middleton condemns acts of cruelty and was quick to stress that he had no idea that they were going to do this, for, if he had, he would never have travelled down to Wales in the first place. Gary, in the vast majority of cases, dug badgers in order to move them for farmers and shepherds, taking them alive and unharmed and releasing them elsewhere. He rarely killed 'Brock', and then only after the insistence of the landowner, if that was required. Badgers do worry livestock and they also carry TB. Also, on occasion, they dig setts out in the middle of fields and cattle, or horses, can fall into them and break their legs, or their digging activities can undermine the foundations of farm buildings, so some farmers were glad to have them removed elsewhere and in a few cases they required them to be destroyed.

Although Lakeland terriers are hard and some attack badgers as they would a fox, it cannot be considered cruel when using such harder terriers. Badgers are incredibly hardy and their pelts are very dense. They have incredibly thick skin too and the vast majority emerged from a dig totally unscathed, for a small dog cannot penetrate the skin of 'Brock'. If a terrier learned how to get to the throat area and it had the power to throttle a badger, then that is the only way in which one could be harmed, but even then it would be a quick death. I have heard of only one terrier that ever managed such a feat and that, as you are now very well aware, was Rex. And so badgers, in the main, do not suffer more than a little irritation and discomfort while being dug. They can take care of themselves and are incredibly quick at striking when defending themselves. In fact, they could strike two or three times before a terrier even knew about it. This tells us something about the game qualities a badger-digging terrier must possess.

Badger digging, in the British Isles, is now illegal, but this practise is still common in places such as France. Of course, it is far better to use baying types when digging badgers, but even these must work their quarry in the right manner. If a terrier goes in and bays from two feet away, 'Brock' will easily move on, or dig himself in further. A terrier must work closely to its quarry, constantly teasing it in order to prevent it from moving, or digging on. This means standing its ground when the quarry charges at it, or nipping at its backside when it attempts to dig. Terriers of this quality were essential to men such as Middleton and in the main he used this sort of a terrier. They were bitten, but not usually too badly and Gary stated that a fox in a bad place very often does more damage than does a badger. True, some of his hard dogs were used for digging badgers, but, like Sid Wilkinson, only in shallow setts from where they could be dug out quickly. Sometimes a dig would work out to be much longer than expected and the harder dog terriers suffered quite a bit of damage in such circumstances, but Middleton did his utmost to ensure that his workers suffered as little damage as possible during badger digs. The earth dog that stands two feet away will be useless when the dig comes to its end, for, when the diggers break through, 'Brock' may charge the terrier and the coward standing at a safe distance will not hold it, or the quarry may have dug itself in. And so a courageous terrier is necessary; one that will stand its ground and seize its quarry in order to hold it in place while the digger tails and bags it. Only the best sort could hope to succeed under such incredibly testing circumstances and Gary, in those days, bred consistently useful badger digging terriers in their droves.

A friend of mine dug badgers with the Middleton strain of Lakeland terrier and he states that they had a knack of seizing 'Brock' by the cheek at the end of digs and drawing him out slowly, slowly, as the diggers finally broke through. He was once high in the Pennines and he entered his dog terrier, Gryke, a typey red dog with a powerful head and resembling Wilk's famous Rock, into an earth just below a long line of crags, thinking a fox was at home. Gryke quickly settled down in one spot, baying constantly, and the digging commenced. Gryke was not a hard terrier, but a strong baying type that would work about half an inch from his foe, nipping and teasing if his quarry attempted to move. He was a superb digging terrier and, though he took a few bites at times, especially if his foe tried to charge past, usually remained unharmed because of cleverly dodging the strikes of his opponent.

As the dig proceeded, John noticed that there was no smell of fox emanating from below, which was unusual, for they often make a stink when being dug out. On breaking through, he found out why. Gryke had bottled up a badger and it had turned its back on him, no doubt attempting to dig on as the terrierman got ever closer to the chamber. After clearing a space, John discovered exactly how his terrier had prevented this from happening. Gryke had actually climbed over the back of the badger and had seized it by the cheek. He had slid down the side of his quarry and was attempting to draw it out backwards as his owner reached him. Gryke, obviously, was a very useful terrier.

Middleton and Brian Fleming with Bracken, Ben and fox taken that day.

Middleton and friends at sett at Witherslack. Group includes Malcolm Lambert and Dave Roberts.

Chad as a pup.

Jessie and Sparky, sired by Punch who worked in Wales.

Whiskey, bought by Brian Meeks, a type very similar to Wilk's Rock.

A good typey terrier bought by Bob and Ruth Arnold.

Trixie drawing 'Brock' at the end of the dig (Winster valley).

Middleton Lakelands popularly known as Johnny D's black and tans.

Chapter Three

ENTERING METHODS

There are several theories concerning methods of entering terriers to foxes and badgers (when badger digging was legal) and there is no end of advice on this subject, but here we will discuss the different ways of entering employed by Gary Middleton himself, over decades of experience. Gary is a traditionalist who expects his dogs to kill reluctant foxes and his bitches to stand off and bay at their quarry, but not from two feet away. He requires a baying type to do its job from half an inch away from its foe and to keep working it in this manner until the fox either bolts, or is dug out.

Some of his bitches, such as the red Trixie mentioned earlier, the dam of Rex, work like dogs and kill foxes, in fact, some are tremendously hard and there have been a number of bitches that could kill foxes very quickly indeed. The majority, though, will stand off and bay, but they work their quarry so hard and work up to it so closely that digging to these Lakelands can be a hair-raising experience, when compared to digging to a traditional Jack Russell that will stand off and constantly bark, nipping and teasing its fox until it decides to make a bid for open ground, or the diggers reach the spot.

Many of these Russells do not even get bitten. I speak from experience, for I have dug to Jack Russells of this type on many occasions and have discovered, upon completing the dig, that the terrier to ground at the time was either uninjured, or it had one or two minor bites. Not so when working Lakeland, or Fell terrier bitches. True, many will not kill a fox, but nevertheless they still work their quarry hard and 'mix it' in order to keep it busy and on its toes, and in doing so they often receive quite bad bites. I have owned bitches of this breed that have even gone jaw to jaw with a fox, especially towards the end of a dig when I have been close to breaking through, and the damage they receive in such circumstances can be pretty horrific. The terrier that avoids the jaw to jaw encounter is the one that will be in active service far more regularly, though a few bites are always inflicted when working foxes so closely.

Fell, a terrier bred by Wendy Pinkney and one that is descended, in part, from Middleton's Ben, another superb worker who could kill a fully grown fox, is a hard fox killer, but he does not go jaw to jaw with foxes. When I bought him, he was a baying type, but he worked his foxes closely at the Pennine Foxhounds and was proving very useful. However, Wendy was overstocked at the time, so she passed him on to myself and I set about working him hard. Our first outing was very fruitful indeed. He went to ground in a small earth on the top of a moor and promptly bolted two reluctant foxes, after a bit of a tangle with them. He proved very useful for digging too and received few injuries. However, as he gained more experience he became harder and eventually began killing foxes by throttling them, rather than tangling with them jaw to jaw. This meant that I could use him week in, week out and he needed few rest periods to recover from injuries. Only occasionally did he need a week or two off work, and then only because I had dug, or bolted, several foxes week after week until, in the end, he needed a bit of time to recover. On the other hand I have had terriers that have needed at least a fortnight of rest after every time they went to ground, because they lacked sense whilst working their quarry. Ghyll was another terrier that received few serious bites, despite the fact that he could kill a fox quickly, once he had closed with it and had got in that fatal throat bite.

Gary states that, in order to produce a hard baying bitch, he enters to fox just below 12 months of age, at maybe ten or eleven months. This often produces a harder bitch that will work closely to its quarry until it either bolts, or is dug out. He says that with dogs, if a hard fox killer is required, he waits to nearer two years of age before he enters them. This makes a lot of sense. If a bitch is entered before it is fully mentally matured, the first bite it receives, if it is game of course, will so enrage the terrier that, from then on, she will work as closely as possible to it, even though she may not have the ability to actually kill a fox. If a dog is allowed to mature mentally by leaving the entering until the approach of the completion of its second year, then a game male will more easily cope with any bites it receives and thus will be in a far better position to close with its quarry and finish it off. This is Middleton's ideal method of entering, but one that was not always put into practise, simply because, in the old days he had that much work on that he needed to bring his youngsters on as soon as possible.

Some of his dogs did not see fox until two years of age, but the majority had worked several badgers by this time and so were easily capable of dealing with the vulpine race in similar circumstances. In fact, because badgers are found to ground all year round and foxes are far more elusive, Gary would always enter to badger first and he had an ideal sett not far from his home that was perfect for the entering of a youngster. The sett remains there and is occupied down to this day, but, obviously, Middleton can no longer use it for the entering of a terrier. At one time he entered the majority of his terriers at this place and most were seasoned badger digging dogs before they saw a fox, but nowadays his terriers are entered straight to fox and work this quarry only. This ideal sett is at Witherslack on the fells above Windermere and has about thirty holes scattered over quite a vast area. It is a testing place and is so big that it allowed a youngster to exercise finding ability and to develop this quality that is so essential in any working terrier, but especially in one that has to work foxes from such terrain that is found in the Lake District.

One may think that such a big place isn't exactly ideal for the entering of a novice, but what makes it so perfect is the fact that the tunnels are only two foot down at the deepest places, only one foot in some areas, and this is because it is a thin layer of soil on top of solid rock. The sett is on the summit of a fell and the rock does not have any hidden grykes or crevices that could mean danger to an inexperienced and unwary terrier. This means that a youngster could be dug out in a relatively short time and thus it was the ideal location for starting a young entry, or for working harder dogs that needed to be dug out quickly in order to avoid more serious injury. Gary, in the earlier days, entered most of his terriers in this place and it was testing indeed.

During those times when badger digging was legal, many would flock to his home in the southern fells and enjoy long, hard digs most Sundays. Ruth, Gary's wife, says that she would spend much time cooking for them on a Sunday and that they would often turn up without notice and she would have to rustle-up countless meals before the dig, and very often afterwards too.

This hunting lark was a little inconvenient for Ruth, especially as she had a young family to raise, and, one day, rather fed up with it all, she asked Sid Wilkinson if Gary would ever give up hunting. "Gary…" He said, pausing and looking rather puzzled, as though he couldn't quite believe she would ask such a question. "Gary.....niver." Was his curt reply. She sighed in resignation of a fate of being married to an obsessive terrierman and duly got on with the job of housewife and mother, knowing that the digging gangs would continue turning up on Sundays. And, oh, what meals she would cook for them. My wife and I have been on the receiving end of her hospitality on several occasions and she cooks a mean full English breakfast.

No wonder those guys were keen on turning up in time for a meal, before going out digging!

One of the chaps who turned up for a badger dig brought a few terriers with him and Gary took him to the large, but shallow, sett on top of a fell at Witherslack. He put one in and it bayed for maybe a quarter of an hour, or twenty minutes, before returning. All were then tried, one after another, and all did more or less the same thing. The chap ran out of terriers in the end and so Middleton, having played the perfect host and allowed the chap to try his dogs first (Gary could dig this place at any time he wished and so didn't mind others having a go), now entered his Lakeland bitch, a blue and tan terrier named Nettle. She was one of his early stock and carried several lines back to Wilk's Rock. She entered the place and began searching through the tunnels, finally bottling up her quarry in a chamber. Gary then dug to his bitch in a relatively short time and uncovered her with 'Brock'.

Nettle was eager to go again and so Gary allowed her another try. Sure enough, another badger was quickly found, bottled up and dug. Yet again, Nettle was keen to go, so she was entered once more, finding and bottling up another badger, until, by late afternoon, Middleton and his digging companion had uncovered five, all dug using the same terrier. As you can imagine, Nettle was exhausted by the end of the fifth dig and had so impressed Middleton's visitor that he bought two pups from Gary before he headed for home.

It was Nettle, when mated by Jock, the son of old Rex, that produced the incredibly game dog, Nailer, the same terrier that George Newcombe, so impressed by the game qualities of this dog who would not give an inch while his quarry lived, used to 'spice up' his strain of working bedlingtons.

Middleton's terriers, in the main, are self-entering and all one has to do is show them a hole. Many working terriers from all breeds are the same and I have seen all different types enter as though they were veterans at the game, but there is possibly not another strain of terrier that so consistently produces self-entering earth dogs. Take Jock, the son of Rex, as an example.

Jock was twelve months old at the time and had never seen a hole before this hunt took place. Gary and his digging companion were hunting the Lythe valley in south Cumbria at the time and a terrier was tried at an earth. It soon returned and so they moved off to try elsewhere. Two or three fields away, Gary loosed Jock to allow him to have a run around and burn off some excess energy and the terrier set off running back the way they had come, heading in the direction of the earth they had just tried. Gary and his mate ran back to the spot and Jock could be heard baying quite some way inside. They started to dig and after a couple of hours or so, they broke through to the terrier. He had bottled up a fully-grown badger and had stayed with it throughout the dig. This was a very good start to a promising career and Jock went on to fulfill this early promise. He was so game that Dave Roberts had him on loan for a while and dug quite a bit of stuff with him. Bill Brightmore also brought Jock into his own strain of terrier when he mated this dog to two of his black bitches. Much of the smarter black stuff today can be traced back to this union, for Brightmore used Middleton's terriers on a few occasions in order to improve both type and working ability in his earth dogs.

The dam of Jock was Candy and she too was a very game worker. She was a daughter of Rock, one of the two terriers returned to Sid Wilk's after they had proven unsuited to a life of domesticity and he, now entered and his boredom cured, became a very game worker to both fox and badger. Candy looked like a dog with a huge head typical of this strain and she was also a very game bitch, capable of killing any fox that would not bolt and not giving an inch when up to a badger.

Middleton was once digging with Gary Hallet and Candy was to ground on a badger, working it, as usual, very hard indeed. When they broke through, the bitch seized her quarry and 'Brock' was tailed and bagged for later release elsewhere. However, they discovered that Candy had a tear in her side, maybe from a badger bite, or maybe from something sharp jutting out into the tunnel, Gary cannot say which, and her intestines were spilling out. In fact, says Gary, they were moving as the bitch bayed and grappled with her quarry. Gary then washed the intestines at a local brook and pushed them back in. She was then taken straight to the vets and her insides were cleaned up and the wound stitched, with antibiotics administered in order to prevent deadly infection of her entrails. Gary has seen some sights and has witnessed scores of demonstrations of how game Lakeland terriers can be, but this was one of the most impressive of all experiences that brought home just how game and hardy they are, for Candy hadn't flinched throughout, in spite of her injuries.

Middleton received dead stock from some of his farmer friends and one rang him and asked if he could pick up a dead calf. Gary went to the farm near Crook, but the farmer wasn't in, so he decided to wait. He took Candy along and his fox killing lurcher, Lucky. He knew of an earth nearby, so he took his terrier to the spot and she entered eagerly. Gary knew this place well and he stated that it was at least six feet deep. His bitch, Candy, then drew a half-grown badger out of one of the holes and Middleton got his terrier to release its hold and then let it go. He now tried another earth nearby and, again, Candy was keen to enter, but this time there were no badgers at home. This time a fox bolted and Lucky was immediately in pursuit, running it down and killing it after only a short distance. Candy followed her fox out, but then immediately turned and went back to earth. She soon had another fox afoot and it too made for open ground, unwilling to face the terrier who would certainly have killed her quarry if it had hung around for too long. Lucky caught and killed his second fox, again, after only a short run.

Candy emerged soon after and Gary made for another earth at the top of a steep bank. Candy entered once more and she could soon be heard at her fox. A few minutes later, a fox ran from the hole and made off down hill, running for a gate into the next field. Lucky chased after his quarry with gusto and, as the fox slipped under the gate, Lucky jumped the obstacle, landing directly behind his quarry and catching and killing it. Meanwhile, another fox emerged, but stood for a few seconds, looking around for danger and failing to see Gary who was slightly behind the earth. And then it bolted when it thought the coast was clear, heading in the same direction as the first fox. Reynard almost ran into the lurcher and Lucky was on it in no time, killing it very quickly.

As the lurcher caught the fox that ran almost right to him, a fox cub popped out of the earth and stood looking down and listening to the sounds of the dog killing the fox. Gary had no intentions of hurting young foxes, so he grabbed it before it could get away, putting it under his jacket. Candy killed the rest of the litter and she returned soon afterwards, having done a good day's work despite the fact that Middleton was only there to pick up a dead calf to feed to his terriers. A half-grown badger had been drawn from an earth, four adult foxes had been bolted and accounted for, together with most of a litter, and a live cub had been saved from the terrier and lurcher, which Gary went on to raise. He showed the farmer his haul and he, of course, was well pleased with the outcome. Had he been in when he arrived, Gary would probably have picked up his dog food and headed for home. Being bored while waiting for the farmer to return, he had decided on a spot of hunting and had been generously rewarded for his troubles.

The fox Middleton had caught outside that earth, saving it from certain death if either Candy or Lucky had caught up with it, settled down well into domestic life and Middleton would often take it to his local pub, the Brown Horse, where it would drink beer out of an ash tray. Gary called his fox Nelson and states that it was as game and as quick as any terrier when ratting. He would sometimes take it to the tip where he would normally use his terriers and he caught many rats using Nelson.

Gary has had some excellent fox catching lurchers over the years and Lucky was one of his best. At the age of two and half years Middleton sold him to a chap in Blackpool and he warned the new owner not to let him off for a few days lest he run off in search of his previous owner. The chap took no notice, however, and a couple of days later Gary received a telephone call saying the lurcher had indeed run off and had simply disappeared. Two weeks later Lucky turned up at Gary's house, looking more than a little dishevelled, having crossed numerous busy roads in order to get back home. Needless to say, Middleton never sold him again and the chap got his money back.

After spending one night in Blackpool for their honeymoon, Gary and his new wife, Ruth, returned home in order to do their cottage up. Middleton had been born and raised at Ann street in Kendal and as a kid the tenants from almost the whole of that immediate area would have the young Middleton on their roofs, shifting jackdaws nests from out of their chimneys. This early 'training' on roofs was to stand Gary in good stead for when he later became a roofer and general builder, though he started off his working life as a coach builder at a garage in Kendal, serving out his apprenticeship and then going on his own. However, the paint fumes became too much for him and he later gave up this type of work, changing to roofing and then building work in general. However, his training as a coach builder provided him with skills he would utilise on many occasions and he sometimes saved farmers such as Anthony Barker, quite a bit of money when he would repair their cars at a fraction of the cost garages charged. Gary now builds carts for horse drives and they are works of art. Again, his early apprenticeship provided the skills needed for this career and most of his income is now earned in this way.

The newly weds lived at Crook, a tiny village 'twixt Windermere and Kendal, for the first few years of their married life, but it wasn't long before they bought what was once a large working farm and set about doing it up, the project lasting for many years. It was whilst working at this place that Lucky was again to demonstrate just how devoted he was to his master. Gary had locked the dog in back at the cottage, but he received a phone call from Ruth as he was busy with different tasks. She said that the lurcher had jumped through the window, smashing a large pane of glass, and had run off. Gary didn't expect the dog to find its way to where he was, for Lucky had never been to the farm before, but shortly afterwards he did indeed turn up on the doorstep of the large farmhouse Gary was working on at the time.

With their new family coming along nicely and neighbours back at Crook beginning to complain because of the noise of the large number of terriers Gary kept, it was decided that it was about time they moved into their new residence and so the Middleton family left the small village and moved into the farm where they still live today. It is a beautiful spot and a place where Gary has had plenty of room for both his business side of life, and his breeding programme for his strain of terrier.

Gary had been breeding his stock at a prolific rate, intent on capturing as much of Wilk's Rock's blood as was possible during those early days, in order to 'lock in' those highly desirable qualities Middleton had so admired in Wilkinson's and Barker's strains of working Lakeland terrier. He bred to Rock himself as much as he possibly could, or to sons of Rock which were found throughout the lakes, not just in the Ullswater country where Rock had become a legendary worker in his own lifetime.

Rock, together with his progeny, showed a quality of gameness that is equalled by few, surpassed by none, and had displayed such courage that, to quote Gary, "he would die in a hole." His offspring were not only constitutionally as hard as iron, with excellent bone structure and superb jackets, but they were also good looking and, more importantly, had proven good finders and, in many cases, were self-entering terriers. Most were fox killers and even many of the bitches grew harder, resembling dogs at their work. And so Gary, even very early on, knew he was on the right track when he settled on this dog as the foundation for his strain of working terrier.

Daughter of Sid Wilkinson's Jock with litter bred early 80s (ph. Bob and Ruth Arnold).

Bill Brightmore with terrier improved by using Middleton bloodlines.

Rex, sold to Brian Meeks, entered to first fox and drew it from the earth.

Tim – a very game terrier.

Judy winning East Lancashire show.

Lucky – superb foxing lurcher.

A terrier sold to Ireland where many Middleton strain Lakelands are at work.

Punch, early 90s. I saw this self-entering terrier at work (ph. Bob and Ruth Arnold).

Chapter Four

THE MIDDLETON STRAIN AND THE SHOWRING

Gary saw a marked improvement in his terrier strain from the very first generation. The working ability improved to such an extent, so early on, that Middleton was very content with what Wilk's Rock was producing, but they still had some way to go with regard to looks. However, one or two of the early terriers were very smart indeed and one of these was Rock, a son of Wilk's Rock. Rock was a very good worker and a very good-looking terrier too and it was with this dog that Gary had his first big win, and possibly his most memorable.

Middleton's Rock was up against some stiff competition, for Tyson, Cowan, Hardasty and Sid Wilkinson all exhibited that day and Rock was up against Hardasty's Turk and Sid Wilkinson's Rock, his own sire, as well as some other very typey earth dogs. George Ridley, Huntsman of the North Lonsdale Foxhounds at the time, was judging and he placed Middleton's terrier above all the others and eventually gave him the championship, and it was then that Gary knew he was on the right track. His dog, Rock, was a very hard terrier, like his sire, and where a fox refused to bolt, he would go in and finish it.

Gary hunted quite a bit with the Lunesdale and the North Lonsdale in those days, as well as the Coniston Foxhounds whenever they were hunting his area of the south lakes, and Rock was well known as a hard fox killer. In fact, Gary's strain were already being talked about throughout the Lake District by this time and few Huntsmen, Walter Parkin excepted, who would always admire a hard terrier and allowed Gary a try whenever circumstances permitted, would let Middleton enter his terrier, for they knew that their quarry would likely be killed. If, however, the fox would not bolt, then Middleton was usually asked to loose his terrier. This niggled him so much that he began to go out less and less with hounds, preferring private digs with friends, shifting foxes and badgers for farmers, shepherds and gamekeepers.

By the third generation Gary was producing something like what he wanted in his strain of terrier. The Dent terriers had proven game and they were hard baying types, working close to their quarry, either fox or badger, and staying until dug out, but there had been something missing in his terriers, which Wilk's Rock put right. By the third generation the majority of his dogs were breeding true to type and were much better looking and far more consistent workers. One of his best wins in those early days was at Lunesdale show when Arthur Irving was judging and he gave Gary the championship. Middleton has much respect for Willie and Arthur Irving, for they consistently bred good working terriers that were also smart enough to compete against anything in the country. The Lake District has a traditional culture of shows and showing and very often terrier shows, together with stick shows, were staged after some of the more important meets, such as shepherds meets held throughout the Lakes. Indeed, many a time has Sid Wilkinson been out digging with Rock, or hunting with hounds, having used the terrier to ground and then returned to the meet venue in order to take part in a show.

Gary takes great pains over preparing his terriers for shows and they are only exhibited when they look their very best. In winter, however, they look pretty much like any other working Lakeland with their scruffy jackets hiding the dog underneath. Middleton tells an interesting tale regarding Wilkinson's Nettle, the dam of his famous dog, Rock. Joe Wilkinson's Rock had been sired by an Egdon terrier, also named Rock, and was a typey black and tan terrier who saw much service at the Ullswater and built quite a reputation for himself as a hard fox killing dog. The dam of Nettle was out of Arthur Irving's famous terrier, Robin, who was bred from Willie Irving's typey stock that helped shape the pedigree Lakeland terrier. So Nettle had quite a pedigree behind her, but Gary was not impressed when he saw the bitch in working condition.

She had a good strong head and was known as a very good worker to fox, but Gary says that she had a scruffy coat at the time of his first seeing her, which was turning blue in colour and betraying a certain amount of bedlington in her bloodlines. On his next visit to Sid's lakeside cottage, Gary saw what he described as a beautiful terrier loose in Sid's garden. Middleton says that this terrier was one of the smartest he has ever seen and stated that it could easily have beaten anything being exhibited at crufts under the guise of 'Lakeland' terrier. He asked Sid about the dog and he was a little taken aback. "Its Nettle." He replied to Gary's enquiries and Middleton couldn't believe it was the same terrier he had seen on his previous visit. Whenever Nettle began turning blue, that was when Sid usually stripped her coat, for she was black and tan when her jacket was not allowed to get too long. Sid was a meticulous sort of chap, says Gary, and his house, his garden with its neat rows of fruit and vegetables for the table, his terriers, indeed, even himself, were usually immaculate. Sid, in fact, led a quiet and well-ordered life and he drank very little, despite some of the hectic celebrations he took part in after a hunt in the Ullswater country. Gary can remember taking him to the White Lion in Patterdale for a drink one night. Sid supped at half a beer, while Gary downed a few pints! Sid was, in essence, the very opposite of his friend, Gary Middleton, who was a wild man who would, I suppose, be classed as a hell-raiser in his younger days, and this may be why their friendship worked so well.

Stripping is best done a few weeks before a big show and is done using a stripping knife. This usually has a short blade and a serrated edge and the fur is gripped using the thumb on the nearside of the blade. The fur should be pulled out in the direction in which it grows, otherwise the job is far more difficult and the poor dog will suffer quite a bit of pain if done the wrong way. Gary has had folk phone him and say that their terrier tries to bite them whenever they strip. He knows immediately why. It is because they are pulling the fur out against the grain, so to speak. For instance, a terrier should be facing away from its master when stripping and the fur should be pulled out towards you, but some are doing it the opposite way; having the terrier facing them and pulling the fur towards them. This hurts the dog and no wonder they try to bite.

Another problem he encounters with folk telephoning is their complaints that their fingers hurt so much that they are going to have to give up stripping. On enquiring how they carry out the job they reply that it is with their fingers. Middleton says that one should always use a stripping knife, for fingers will hurt when used in this way. The blade makes the job so much easier and the user suffers far less discomfort when stripping out a terrier in preparation for a show. Gary will also rub the coat with a little bit of chalk before stripping, just to remove some of the grease from the coat, which makes it easier to grip in the first place. The top-coat should be pulled out until there is just the almost smooth undercoat left and, when the top-coat begins growing through again, it will become iron hard and very rich in colour.

It is very important to strip a coat, rather than cut it with scissors, or, worse still, shave it with clippers, for this will soften the coat and will turn it a much lighter colour. Black will become a very wishy-washy colour, while a red terrier will turn blonde. This poor colour and softened coat will mean that the terrier will do very badly in shows. Some will clip the coat of a russell type if it is poor to begin with and the short jacket will come back a little harder and wiry, but it won't last for long. Stripping is always the best method to use for a working terrier in order to produce as hard a coat as it is possible to do so. Some have iron hard jackets that are at their very best after stripping, while some coats are quite poor to start with. Stripping out in the spring of each year may help to improve the coat, but a naturally poor coat can only be improved so much by stripping. Gary strips the jacket once a year, but will continue gently pulling out any long, or dead hairs, as the summer show season progresses. For stripping he uses the knife, while for keeping the coat tidy he uses another tool with a serrated edge that pulls out long and dead hairs (the following photographs show stripping in progress with a before and an after shot, as well as the tools used for this task).

It is vital to strip the coat at the time one thinks best, possibly a few weeks before a big show so that time is allowed for the top coat to begin growing through again, if the chances of winning at shows are to be maximised. Poor coats are quite a bad fault on a terrier. A working terrier can still function properly with legs that are not quite straight, or a back that may be a little too long, but a terrier with a poor jacket is at risk whilst working during midwinter, especially in places such as the English Lake District. Many of the earths are in rock and there is little warmth to be had whilst working such places, so good jackets are essential on Lakeland terriers and nothing less will do. Stripping only improves the coat, for when it gets long and untidy the jacket is an unsightly mess that should not be seen in a showring. Gary tells an interesting tale that illustrates just how effective stripping can be when showing terriers.

Middleton was at the Melbreak show one year when one of his acquaintances offered him the chance to buy a terrier at just £40.00. The red terrier wasn't up to much and was not in show condition, but there was something about it that Gary took to, so he took the chap up on the offer and bought it. Middleton then took it behind his van and stripped it out until he had a dog that was fit for the showring. He entered it and won his class, beating the original owner's dog, which was placed 3rd. The chap who had sold it then asked where he had got his terrier from and Gary informed *him* that it was the dog he had just bought from him. He couldn't believe the transformation and was rather 'sick' that he had been beaten by his own rejected dog. Gary let him have the rosette, however, but then went on to sell the terrier for £150.00 at the same show!

P. 79-86 show before, stripping and after shots, and tools used.

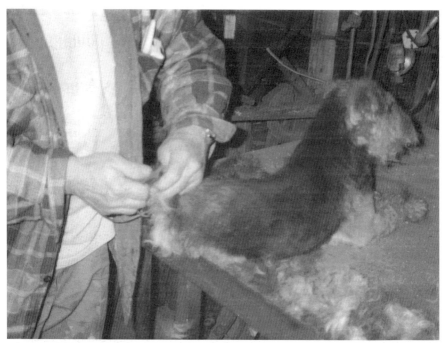

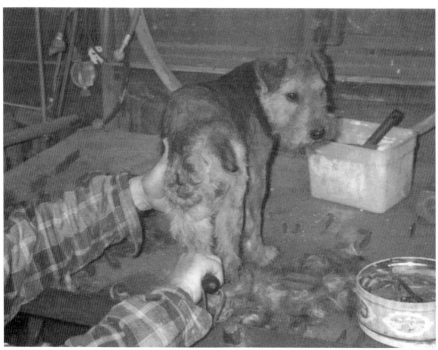

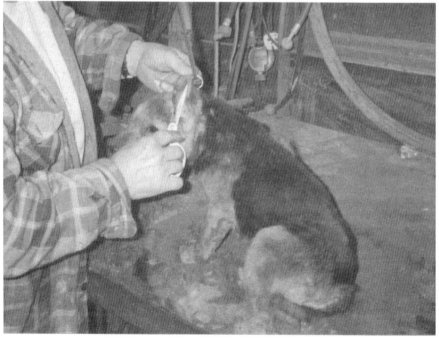

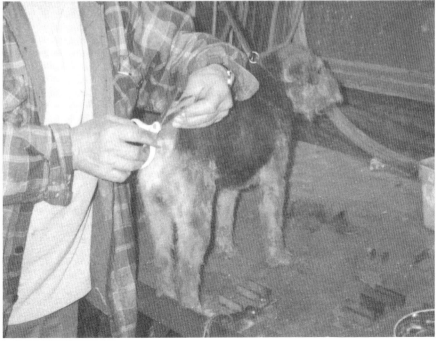

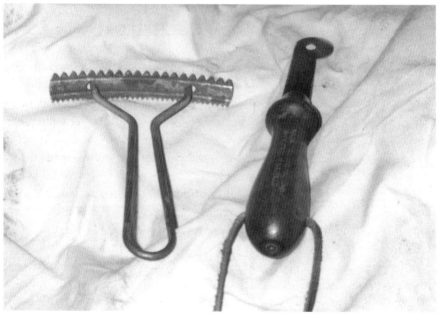

On another occasion Gary was at a show in Wales and a chap was trying to sell a terrier for just £50.00, but he had no takers. Middleton went to look at the terrier which was in the back of the van. Again, the coat was long and scruffy and the dog didn't look to be of any quality whatsoever, but Gary had much experience with terriers by this time and he could see something in the dog that made him buy it. He handed over his £50.00 and, again, took the terrier out of sight and stripped it out. He was pleased with his purchase, for the dog was really quite typey and generally of good quality. Gary entered his new acquisition in the show and went on to win it, taking the championship too. He then sold the dog at the same show for £300.00 to a chap who had had the chance of buying it for just £50.00 earlier that day, though Gary kept quiet about that!

Gary Middleton has been breeding, working and exhibiting terriers for over fifty years now and, as one can imagine, he has become a very good judge of a terrier and his skills are in much demand. What he is looking for in a terrier, whilst both exhibiting and judging, are qualities that make the dog pleasing to the eye, while being suited to work below ground. He likes to see quite a large head on a terrier with a powerful jaw and a natural scissor-bite. Undershot and overshot mouths are faulted and one would do badly at most shows with terriers that had these faults, though this would also depend on the quality of the other exhibits. He likes to see plenty of reach in the neck area, for a terrier will lunge, dodge and dart while at work and a good reach and plenty of strength in the neck will be a great advantage, though a long neck, more akin to a whippet, is not desirable.

Gary likes a short back, but not so short that the chest almost reaches to the back legs. The chest must have plenty of room for strong heart and lungs, but it must not be too deep, again, more akin to whippet blood, or too barrel-shaped, more akin to bull terrier blood. Both a barrel chest and a very deep one, will hamper a terrier working underground. A short-coupled, square dog is favoured by judges of Lakeland terriers, but this must be of a natural short length where movement and agility is not restricted. He likes a hard double coat on a terrier, a softer undercoat for insulation and a harsh outer coat that helps shed water, snow and ice. The jacket must be dense too, giving plenty of protection from icy winds; one of the worst killers of working terriers in mountainous regions.

The terrier should have tight feet that can give plenty of grip on rocks and rough ground. The skin must be thick and the terrier must have substance, in other words it must have good bone structure and not be so light in weight that it would blow away in a strong wind. The terrier must also be easily spannable. This is essential for working the borran earths of Cumbria and North Yorkshire – the birthplaces of fell and Lakeland terriers. The legs should be straight and the general type well balanced. The neck should not look too long, or the back, or the legs. True, Gary likes a bit of leg on a terrier in order to aid it in crossing rough country – an essential quality in hilly and mountainous districts, but not so much that they almost look like a mini-lurcher. A strong, well-rounded terrier is what Gary favours; one that could handle itself and stand its ground against the large fell foxes this breed was created to hunt. The actual size of a terrier he favours is 13-14 inches at the shoulder for a dog and 12-13 inches for a bitch, though he does not decry a larger terrier and has bred some very good ones. I have owned a couple of larger Middleton bred Lakelands and they could not be faulted for courage, or looks, though they struggled to work some of the smaller earths.

There is a school of thought that says that you cannot have both top winning terriers that also work very well. This is seen often at shows with battle-scarred ugly terriers, full of obvious faults, being put up before much smarter stuff in 'entered terrier' classes, as though the judge cannot accept that a smarter dog could possibly work. Old Rex won the Great Yorkshire show, among many others, and would compete well against anything today, but only a fool would question the gameness of this terrier and the working qualities he passed on to his progeny, which can be numbered in hundreds, thousands if grandsons and granddaughters were to be included. Rex would sooner have died than backed down from either fox or badger and was known to kill two and three foxes in one day's hunting on more than one occasion (this is verified by those who saw this terrier at work). There are plenty of witnesses who can vouch for the game qualities of the Middleton strain of terrier and they both look well, competing against all the best terriers throughout the country, and work well too.

What many folk do not know is that Gary has an army of terrier lads who queue up to buy his stock. These lads despise shows and would never even think of exhibiting, but they use Middleton strain Lakeland terriers for fox bolting and digging week in, week out throughout the season, and this suits Gary very well indeed. While lads are buying and using stock in this way, while not showing, they are helping to keep the working qualities in the strain, but are not competing against Gary whenever he exhibits his terriers. He doesn't really mind too much when his own strain beats his dogs at shows, but he much prefers to sell most of his pups to digging lads, and these are found throughout the British Isles, as well as in Ireland, Canada and America. Many of his top winning terriers have also been first class workers and Rex is possibly the ultimate example of this, though Toby, a more recent terrier and a grandson of Rex, is another fine example of a terrier that both looks, and works, very well indeed.

Toby was another very hard terrier and he killed many foxes during his lifetime. Also, like his grandsire, he produced hard fox killing offspring that also did very well in the showring. One of his best known pups was Tyke, owned by Desie Makin, which won a lot of top shows, but he was also a very good worker too. Gary's present stud dog, Rex, was sired by Toby and he is an incredibly typey terrier who is also a hard fox killer, having lost all of his top teeth whilst engaging his quarry.

Rex has sired plenty of top winning show terriers such as Andrew Meeks Sam who is, again, a very good worker. In fact, Brian and Andrew Meeks have smartened their own strain of terrier using Middleton blood and these have proven very good workers too. Brian and Andrew Meeks are yet more examples of those who know how to produce both good looking and good working stock and only a fool would question the abilities of such terriers.

Rex has also sired Boss, a black and tan terrier bred by Bob and Ruth Arnold that is a replica of his sire and Boss is proving game indeed. He entered to the very first fox he saw and killed it, at just ten months of age. He is also very smart and has won many puppy championships. By the time of the next show season he will be in the adult classes and will have had a full season of work behind him.

Those who say that Middleton stock does not work are kidding themselves, and those who listen to such nonsense. In fact, a red terrier Gary recently bred, one he showed three times in the puppy section and won all three championships, including Lowther, has just gone up to a village on the outskirts of Glasgow and he too entered to his first fox, working it hard for the last twenty minutes of the dig.

He looks very promising indeed and will see plenty of work during the next season and those to come afterwards and no doubt Gary will bring the blood of this dog back into his strain, for he is a good looker and has a resemblance of Wilkinson's Rock. Rock himself is the ultimate example of a terrier that can work very well indeed, while being very typey and a top winning show terrier. A better worker than Rock would be very hard to find, believe me.

During those early days Gary had quite a few problems with poor colour, for this is another important quality in a Lakeland terrier. Black and tan, or red, are the favoured colours, but, because of a strong bedlington and fox terrier influence, some of his puppies were coming with blue and fawn coats, or a poor wishy-washy black and tan.

Gary needed to put this problem right if he was to enjoy a consistently successful show career, but he had problems as to how to go about this. Some say that Middleton used pedigree Welsh terrier blood in order to produce the rich black and tan that his strain is famous for, or, indeed, pedigree Lakeland terrier blood, but that simply isn't true. We can certainly rule out pedigree Lakeland blood, for poor colour is a fault found in this breed to this day, so Middleton would have been a fool if he had resorted to such blood that would only have aggravated the existing problem.

Before embarking on writing this book, which, I believe, is an important record that must be written down now, before this vital information is lost forever, I wanted to be sure that Gary would be honest with me. I had heard rumours of this pedigree Welsh terrier having been brought into the Middleton strain in order to improve colour and so I touched on the subject, asking him outright if he had ever used such blood.

Gary could simply have denied that he had, for he tries to keep his bloodlines pure and does not wish to bring into his strain anything that is not related to Wilk's Rock, but he didn't deny this at all and was completely honest with me. On this occasion, he simply had no choice, but the terrier used, he was quick to stress, was not a pedigree Welsh.

It was early in his breeding programme that, at the Kendal and District Otterhounds show, Gary met up with a Mr Williams who was a friend of Major Roche of the Ynsfor hounds. Gary sold Mr Williams a red bitch and was invited down to Wales in order to help shift badgers that were proving troublesome in that area.

Gary went down for two days, taking with him Rags, a red bitch, and Rags, a black and tan dog who was a son of old Rex. Rags, the dog, was incredibly game, but the bitch was a better finder and would probably be a granddaughter of Wilk's Rock.

They dug twenty badgers in those two days from well used setts, digging eight out of one hole and taking some from a hole that was actually dug into the sea wall. Major Roche and Mr Williams then bought quite a few terriers from Gary and they served at the hunt kennels for several years. The reason for this story is that, while Gary was spending quite a bit of time digging foxes and Badgers in different regions of Wales, he met a chap who bred

Rex and his son Boss, who entered to and killed first fox at ten months (ph. Bob and Ruth Arnold).

The red dog winning Lowther, before heading off to Scotland (ph. Bob and Ruth Arnold).

After winning champion pup at Lowther '05, this red dog entered to its first fox during a dig in Scotland (ph. Pauline Middleton).

Toby, looker and worker and sire of Desie Makin's Tyke and Neil Stobbart's Twist.

Hoot, a game terrier, but with the poor blue and fawn colouring.

Rex at Lowther '99, very game, typey and with good colour.

his own strain of working Welsh terrier which were very good looking and was also incredibly game. Gary believes these were probably from the same rootstock that gave rise to the pedigree Welsh terrier, but he is also pretty certain that fell blood had also been used on this strain, for they were very similar to good classy unregistered Lakeland terriers of a type the Irving brothers and the Wilkinson family had been breeding for many years.

He can't quite remember the name of the chap, but he thinks he was a Mr Snow and he lived in the Seven Sisters area. He had a number of terriers and they were of a deep black and rich tan colouring, the very same colours, in fact, Gary needed in order to correct the faults in his own terrier strain. True, only a small proportion of his stock came with poor colour, but he knew that, in years to come, if he did not correct it now, those faults would become more pronounced as the gene pool lessened somewhat. So he had to act. He bought a black and tan bitch from this strain and named her Judy (Gary has used the same names for his terriers over the years and so it is difficult to know which terriers he is talking about). She was very typey and game, for Gary tested her to the full *before* bringing her into his strain of Lakeland terrier.

He dug many fox and badger using this bitch and, now fully convinced that Judy was game, having proven a good finder and stayer too, Gary brought her into his own strain of Lakeland terrier and she was mated by old Rex. Rex himself was of good colour, being black and tan, and it was hoped that the influence of this Welsh bitch would eliminate the wishy-washy coloration that was proving troublesome at this point. This union produced four puppies and Gary kept one himself, a black and tan bitch he also called Judy, while the others were bought by a chap from Birmingham.

Gary saw these at a later date and he said that they were very smart indeed, though he didn't breed from any of them, just the bitch he had kept back. A lot of good quality black and tan terriers being worked and shown today can be traced back to this union and the Welsh Judy is the great grandam of Middleton's current stud dog, Rex, who is a veteran of ten years at the time of writing, though he remains very typey and is still game enough to kill a fox.

Like Wilk's Rock, he too is producing excellent quality pups in old age and his stuff is also very game, the dogs he produces usually turning out to be hard fox killers.

Gary has won up and down the country with his typey Lakeland terriers and he has also worked them in every country of the British Isles. His championship wins are too numerous to recount and his hauls of rosettes are numbered in thousands, rather than hundreds. In fact, I would confidently say that Gary Middleton is *the* most successful exhibitor of dogs outside of crufts this country has ever produced. He has no scientific background, being a coach builder, roofer, general builder, dry stone waller and now a builder of carts for horse drives, but he is one of the cleverest of all dog breeders and knows exactly what he wants and how to go about getting it. And, what is more, he can breed both a good-looking terrier and an excellent worker, and has been doing so consistently for the past few decades; something few could achieve. True, his terriers are no longer tested as to gameness in the same manner as in previous years when Middleton was a passionate badger digger, but they remain excellent fox dogs and many are hard to the point of being almost suicidal. He recently sold a bitch terrier to a chap in Bolton and, once she was entered, Gary received a phone call saying that the bitch was too hard. The chap who had bought her required a baying type and many of Middleton's bitches are such, but this one worked more like a traditional dog terrier and just didn't suit what was required of her, so Gary bought her back and sold her to a chap in Ireland where she is building quite a reputation as an excellent worker. Another terrier that made quite a name for itself was a white-legged Lakeland who was a brother of Tyke and Twist, sons of the illustrious Toby, which went to Kent and became an incredible worker, becoming very hard to the point where few foxes could manage to bolt, even if they wanted to. White-footed Rocky was another of Middleton's terriers that made a name for itself in more recent years. He was bred out of Jock, the son of Rex who was a superb worker and also a very good looker, and Trouble, a typey bitch which was very game indeed. Stuart Sims of Barnsley bought this dog and he dug plenty of stuff using Rocky.

Even though they are not tested on badgers anymore, which many regard as the ultimate test of a terrier's abilities, the dogs and bitches must prove themselves on foxes before they are used for breeding and Gary will not breed from a dog that cannot kill a fully grown fox. Cyril Breay also lived by this rule and he was another who succeeded in producing good working and looking stock. Gary does not favour the type of terrier Cyril Breay bred, but he freely admits that many of them were very good looking indeed, such as Bingo and, according to Gary, one of his best was Skiffle, a black bitch which sometimes beat Wilk's Rock and Hardasty's Turk in the showring.

Gary dug with Cyril Breay on a number of occasions and the old gentleman sometimes brought young terriers to the Winster valley where

Gary would help in entering them for the first time on badger digs in this area. He can remember two very game black terriers which Breay entered on digs with Gary, though he cannot remember their names. Middleton has also dug badgers with Breay around the Kirkby Lonsdale area where Breay taught at Casterton school. Bingo was one of his best and he was not only very smart, but he was also incredibly hard and would not leave an earth while a fox lived. Gary was out with the Lunesdale foxhounds when they were hunting the Lythe valley in south Cumbria.

They had hunted a fox and put it to ground in a massive rock spot that was utterly impossible to dig. This place is a massive outcrop of rock with a hole at one end and another at the opposite end, which is hundreds of yards away. The Huntsman knew it would be a tall order bolting a fox from this place and so he wished for a hard terrier to be used. Breay was asked to try Bingo, for he had already built up an almost legendary reputation as a worker, and the terrier entered this vast den. Only the best of finders could hope to succeed in such a place as this and Bingo was obviously of good quality in every department, not just as a killer of foxes, for he soon found his fox and tackled it hard. His quarry would not bolt, no matter how hard Bingo worked it, so in the end, as one would expect, Bingo killed the fox below ground. When Bingo emerged he was in a sorry state. As Gary put it, he was 'absolutely blattered' when he came out of there. Foxes are tough fighters and can give a good account of themselves, especially when they find a good vantage point from which to strike. Middleton has much respect for the memory of Cyril Breay, for he was a good breeder of quality terriers that could both work well and win at working terrier shows.

Gary respects the views of those who are happy to breed terriers of any type, whether typey or otherwise, as long as they work, but he requires a terrier to be pleasing to the eye, as well as to be very game and hardy. He only asks for the same respect accorded to others and not to be criticised just because his dogs are good looking and win well at shows.

Lookers and workers, Middleton's terriers with dead fox.

Trouble, looker and worker. She won this Welsh show three years running.

Becky, daughter of Rex (Aug '05). The influence of Wilkinson's Rock can clearly be seen all these years later (ph. Bob and Ruth Arnold).

Boss, son of Rex and hard terrier (ph. Bob and Ruth Arnold).

P. 99-100 – just some of the trophies won by Middleton's terriers.

Just some of the rosettes won by Middleton's terriers.

Thousands of rosettes, though there were more.

Middleton with rosettes piled almost to his elbow.

Rex, a veteran at ten years, but still game and typey.

Chapter Five

THOUGHTS ON BREEDING

After fifty four years of breeding terriers and after decades of breeding a strain that is relatively pure and has been breeding true to type for much of that half a century, I think Gary Middleton is more than qualified to give some of his own thoughts on breeding terriers and some of the dogs he has produced over the years, with a few more pointers on showing, judging and working. And the reader would do well to take note, for Gary has not only worked every large quarry species in the British Isles with his strain of Lakeland terrier, but he has also won every major show, together with hundreds of smaller venues, sometimes several times over, up and down the country.

A bitch terrier of the working Lakeland type should never be bred from until it has proven game. Gary never breeds from inferior stock and tests it before breeding, though foxes are the hardest quarry his terriers now see. At one time they would have been used to dig several badgers and foxes before breeding occurred, but nowadays, of course, foxes are the only larger quarry his youngsters can be tested on, though even that is limited, after the ban in 2005 which states that terriers can only be used to ground on foxes where birds are reared, or preserved, for shooting, and then only after written permission has been obtained. Middleton can visit friends in Scotland and Ireland, however, where terriers can be worked with much more freedom.

Before breeding from either a dog, or bitch, they must meet certain standards. The bitch must, of course, have proven game, baying close up to her fox and staying until the quarry either bolts, or is dug out. She must also prove to be a good finder. She must be of good conformation and preferably of good colour, either red or black and tan, and her preferred size is around twelve or thirteen inches.

The stud dog must also prove game and if he bays, rather than kills his fox, then, to Gary, he does not measure up to the traditional standard of a Lakeland dog terrier and he will not be used, but be sold on to fox diggers. The stud dog must measure up to this standard simply because he is the one who can produce many pups and in the old days outstanding males, such as Wilk's Rock, Anthony Chapman's Twist, Joe Wear's Tear 'Em and Cyril Breay's Bingo, would be used on every game bitch in their hunt country, as well as beyond, in order to produce the very gamest of stock. This proved true of all the males mentioned and Eddie Pool states that Cyril Breay and Frank Buck brought bitches to Wear's Tear'Em and that his blood then entered into their strain of terrier now known as Patterdales. Eddie can clearly remember Tear'Em being used by Buck and Breay and they then went on to use a son of Tear'Em, his bloodlines meant so much to them (see Plummer's *The Fell Terrier*). In fact, this dog was such an outstanding fox killer that Gary is certain his blood entered the Wilkinson and Barker strains during the forties and early fifties when Tear'Em served at the Ullswater hunt. Certainly, Anthony Barker, valuing the abilities of the strain of terrier bred by Jim Fleming of Grasmere, used a sister of Tear'Em to bring into his own strain of terrier. Tear'Em had a massive head and this may have helped cement this quality that Gary has tried so hard to preserve. A large head and powerful jaws are essential to Gary on any stud dog, for he believes they need such in order to tackle a big hill fox, though he has seen some good smaller terriers that were death to foxes, terriers with small heads and snipey jaws. Again, the dog must be of good conformation, more or less the same qualities he would look for in one of his exhibits, or when judging. Size for a dog is ideally around the thirteen or fourteen-inch mark, though he breeds some good ones that are a shade smaller, or even a little larger. Of course, coat is important and both the dog and bitch must have harsh wiry jackets that repel bad weather.

A bitch will usually be ready for mating from the ninth or tenth day after bleeding begins and many books state that two matings are best. This is indeed true, but it is a rule Gary doesn't go by. He puts a stud to the bitch just once, for he says that if you mate more than that, then you are unsure of the exact date of impending birth and you then do not know if a bitch is early or late, and he prefers to know the exact date just in case of any complications. He will have his bitch mated on either the thirteenth or fourteenth day of her heat. A week before the bitch is due to whelp her pups, Gary puts plenty of fresh straw in the kennel and this gives a bitch time to chew it up so that the bed is ready for the new arrivals. If the bitch has plenty of milk, he will wean at around four weeks of age, otherwise he weans at three weeks, keeping the pups with their dam for a few weeks after this, and Ruth, his wife, liquidizes a complete puppy food for the first week, after which they have it as normal. Docking takes place at three days and this must now be done by a vet, according to law, though Middleton's methods have worked very well for years before this law was passed. He simply uses a pair of scissors for cutting off the tails, leaving just over half on, and then puts the bitch back with them once they have settled, which takes no time at all. During the actual procedure, he has the bitch well away from her youngsters so that she does not become at all distressed. He says that it is pointless dipping the tails in anything, for the bitch licks it off immediately anyway, and has no problems with bleeding, for this stops very quickly. A vet will use a silver nitrate stick to stop the bleeding immediately and this is very effective indeed, though, as Gary says, in the scheme of things it really isn't necessary, for blood loss is minimal. The pups obviously feel something when the tails are docked, but not very much at all, for they will settle very soon after the job is done and show no signs of distress thereafter. He believes that docking is essential for working terriers, not only because of what judges are looking for in the showring, but because tails can be damaged while at work. However, dewclaws are left on, for these, says Gary, are vital tools used while at work for scaling the sides of earths. I can only agree with what he says. Some working terrier folk will say that dewclaws should be removed and I cringe every time I hear this, for I have often noticed my terriers using this appendage whilst at work, especially for scaling smooth rocks, or a wet and slippery stone floor of a drain, so it was good to hear Gary telling of the importance of dewclaws.

The use of dewclaws was noticed very early on in Gary's career as a working terrier enthusiast when he took part in a hunt near Crook. Tiny, one of his early bitches that was used to breed several of Rock's offspring, was incredibly game and a very good finder and she saw plenty of work at both fox and badger. One day Gary and his companion tracked two foxes in the snow and they followed their prints to a rock earth, which isn't far from the Sun Inn at Crook. This is a bad place and is a sort of natural chimney in the rock, which goes right down into the ground. The two foxes were obviously still in here, for no prints exited the den, and so Tiny was loosed from the couplings. The little bitch entered carefully and managed to climb down the fissure and soon disappeared into the bowels of the earth.

The bitch soon found the pair of skulking vulpines, deep inside that rock spot, and engaged them. It wasn't long before both bolted, fleeing from the wrath of the small earth dog, and they were both shot and killed instantly, but the bitch was unable to follow her quarry out. The sides of this earth are worn smooth and it is a difficult place. True, she had managed to climb down, sometimes sliding down the rocks for some distance, but simply could not return that way. After thinking about how to go about freeing his bitch and attempting to effect a rescue over two days, Gary decided to cut a bough from a nearby yew tree, which he then dropped into the earth. After some encouragement, Tiny began making attempts to climb out and she eventually made progress by digging her dewclaws into the sides of the bough and climbing out that way. It had been a close call and a seriously long and tedious rescue attempt had only just been avoided, but Gary got his bitch out of there and ever since then has been fully convinced of the need to leave dewclaws on puppies.

He will not use a bitch for work when she is well into her pregnancy, for fear of her becoming trapped and the rescue taking some time before a successful outcome is reached. Gary cites a case of a seventeen day dig that had started when a fox was marked to ground in a big place near Cockermouth. Rags, a red bitch bred out of Tim, a tidy looking dog who was very game and who was a son of Wilkinson's Rock, was entered into this earth and it soon became obvious that Reynard was not going to bolt. Maybe the fox could not bolt, for Rags was a hard bitch and she killed several foxes during her lifetime.

The place was so deep that the bitch could not even be heard at work and after some time and worry, and plenty of digging by hand, more or less guided by educated guesswork (this was long before locators came on the scene), a mechanical digger was brought in and over several days moved tons of rock and earth. By the seventeenth day, things were looking very bad and spirits were low. Rags had proven a very useful worker to both fox and badger and Gary was more than a little upset at the thoughts of losing such a good terrier, but it all seemed hopeless by now and everybody was ready to give up.

When events were at their lowest ebb and the digging about to be abandoned, an old chap walked over to the scene with his pet Jack Russell terrier at his side. Middleton stated that he favoured Alf Garnett and he wondered if the old chap was going to take exception to what they were doing, but he was simply enquiring as to what was going on and Gary told him. By this time the digger had dug out a massive hole and the old gent said that he would have a go. "She'll find it." He said, confidently pointing at his dog, and then, with some difficulty, climbed down into the hole and allowed his Jack Russell to sniff around.

The terrier then began scratching at a place on the side of the dig and the old chap poked it with his stick and opened up a small hole. "It'll be in 'ere." He said, but the diggers were not too optimistic, as not too many pet Jack Russells had made a name for themselves in the Lake District. However, there was now some hope where there had previously been none and so they set to and began following this hole. They dug in and after around six foot or so they came upon a dead fox, but there was only half of it left. Rags then emerged and she was not the terrier they expected to find. After so long to ground they expected to find her near dead from starvation, possibly even dead, but she was 'as fat as a pig' says Gary and in general good health, though she had gone temporarily blind. This only lasted a few days, however, and she was soon back to full health. If a pregnant bitch was trapped for so long and it didn't have a carcass to feed upon (terriers will sometimes become trapped after bolting a fox), then great damage could be done to pups, as well as the bitch, and they would possibly be lost.

The terriers he breeds from must also work their foxes with sense and for this reason Gary avoids bull terrier blood in the studs he chooses. Middleton has a lot of respect for the terriers of Cyril Breay and he has dug with quite a number of them, stating that they were certainly very game workers, but that some of them lacked sense. He has uncovered Breay's terriers and they have had the fox by a paw, or the brush, or a leg, refusing to let go despite their victims retaliating and punishing them severely. This, Gary believes, is irrefutable evidence of bull terrier blood having played a part in the creation of the Buck/Breay strain and he sometimes put this to Mr Breay, for Middleton knew him well and hunted with him on several occasions. In fact, it was Gary who took Mr Breay on possibly his very last dig just before he died. Whenever Gary asked him about the use of bull terrier blood, Mr Breay simply smiled a mischievous smile, but would say nothing!

As with any strain of terrier, faults do crop up on occasion and a few of Middleton's terriers have grown to be undershot. Gary says that the majority with this fault had very large heads and square, powerful jaws, which, he believes, betrays bull terrier blood in the distant ancestry. All breeds of terrier originate from a mix that includes old bulldog and bull terrier blood and this, he says, is where the fault comes from.

Of course, not all with large heads and powerful jaws have this fault, for old Rex and Wilk's Rock himself, as well as bitches such as Trixie, Jewel and Rags, had ''eads like a brick' and were without this annoying problem, but Gary occasionally has problems with this fault. And, no matter how game the dog or bitch, or even how typey it is, he will not breed from it. He will sell it on to fox diggers and he has plenty of takers when one of his terriers comes on the market, which tells the reader something of the abilities of this strain. Gary gets plenty of publicity and takes some stick because he wins a lot of shows, or because people who keep and breed his terriers do so, for some seem to think that top winning terriers just cannot make the grade as workers. What rubbish. I know of several lads who never show, but they keep Middleton strain Lakelands and take plenty of foxes with them. In the old days, when it was legal, some used these for digging badgers and better 'holders' of a large boar badger could not be found. Of course, this 'won't give ground' sort of disposition means that quite a number of these terriers died whilst working 'Brock' and a number were badly injured at fox, but still, they could not be faulted for sheer courage and that still holds good today. I have come across a number of folk who proudly boast that their terriers go back 'to Middleton's old stuff', usually citing old Rex as the ancestor of their strain.

In fact, much of the black stuff around today has Middleton blood running through their veins, through the terriers of Bill Brightmore and Barry Wild, among others, and no-one questions the working abilities of their strains. Yet, Gary is credited with breeding non-workers, despite the fact that all of his present stock is closely related to all of his 'old stuff', Rex in particular. Others have brought Middleton's terriers into their own strains and improved them by doing so, yet they do not breed the same pure bloodlines that is all closely related to Sid's old Rock, so why do they think that Middleton's stock are not workers? It is a baffling enigma and there are plenty of working terrier lads, and I mean serious digging enthusiasts, who can testify to the fact that the Middleton strain is still very much a working terrier.

While Gary will avoid breeding from a terrier with a serious fault, in order to breed away from this, he will breed extensively from those that display good looks, few minor faults and, essentially, good working ability. He does this by breeding related stock in order to keep his bloodlines pure. The fact that several of his youngsters, even today, closely resemble Wilkinson's Rock, is evidence enough that Gary has kept close to the original bloodlines. He will not breed too close, though, for that would create problems with faults and deficiencies, even abnormalities. He bred very close early on, occasionally putting Rock to his own daughters and granddaughters, but Gary is cautious about such tactics now as all his stock is related and so he must avoid breeding too close to the line.

He has created a large enough gene pool that enables him to keep breeding from related stock simply because he bred so many important stud dogs that were sons and grandsons of Rock, as well as brood bitches, all of which are also related to the old Dent strain. Rex, Tim, Chip, Rags, Rock, Jock, among many others, were very important studs and all proved game when up to fox, or badger. Chip is the terrier that is the subject of our introduction and Gary states that he was bred out of Trixie, a red bitch which closely resembled Wilk's Rock and could kill any fox that refused to bolt, and his sire was a son of Rock which was owned by a chap at Hartsopp Hall, another very game Lakeland. Trixie also bred Rex, when put back to Rock. Rex sired the black and tan Rags and then, when put to Candy, he produced Jock, who then sired Nailer - the same who was used as outcross blood for George Newcombe's strain of working bedlington. Jock, when put to Trouble, a top winning black and tan bitch, bred white-footed Rocky and he in turn produced Middleton's Jock, another extremely hard fox killer that once took part in a rather curious hunt.

Hounds had been hunting a fox around the lower fells of south Cumbria and eventually ran it to ground. The pack had got well ahead of hunt servants and followers, but they were marking at a drain when the Huntsman arrived with the terriers. Three were tried and all failed to find anything in that earth and it was decided that the fox must have run the drain and then emerged, heading off elsewhere, which is something that occasionally happens when hunting in the fells, or in the shires for that matter.

I was once out with the Coniston foxhounds and they had roused a fox from Loughrigg fell, which they then proceeded to hunt for two or three hours down into the Langdale valley. I lost them for quite some time, but eventually heard hounds returning, pressing their fox hard. They eventually followed scent to the back face of Loughrigg and soon began marking at a drain close to the foot of the fell. A terrier was tried, but it simply ran through and hounds managed to pick up the scent again and follow their fox out onto the open fell top. That fox had managed to throw hounds off its scent for a while and it was able to gain enough ground so that it secured its brush for that day.

The Huntsman now moved his pack on from this drain in order to try for another, as hounds couldn't pick up a line, being adamant that Reynard was indeed at home. One of the followers, once the hunt had moved on and being one of Middleton's many friends, telephoned Gary and told him of hounds marking, believing there to be a fox at home and the terriers, maybe because they were inexperienced, just couldn't find their quarry (some drains are not straightforward and can be difficult places for terriers to work, especially if young and rather green at the game). Gary took Jock along and met up with his friend. Jock was keen to go at the drain and, sure enough, he found a fox skulking in the tunnel below a dry-stone wall. He then seized his quarry and had killed it by the time Gary and his companion broke through, digging as close to the wall as it was possible to do. Jock, like his sire and grandsire, was a wonderful worker who could both find and kill foxes and Gary took many using this terrier. His sire, White-Footed Rocky, went on to make a grand name for himself around the Pennine districts of Lancashire and West Yorkshire and many terriers are descended from this dog. I once saw one of his descendants at work in a rockpile at an old quarry and he was most impressive, despite him being on the larger side. He also carried the same markings, having a couple of white paws and a touch on his legs and chest. He had a large head and could kill a fox that would not bolt. He ended up working with hounds in Cheshire and performed well in this role. I cannot quite remember his name, but I am pretty certain he was called Jock.

Many terrier enthusiasts have used Middleton strain blood in order to improve working ability in their stock, as well as to make them more competitive in the showring. Gary states that, unless they then line breed, these improvements will soon be lost. Unscientific breeding produces some good stuff, there can be no doubt about that, but by putting anything to anything one could produce anything; in other words, one would not know the results of such breeding and a litter could be a variety of types, with some looking like bedlingtons, while others look like old fashioned Yorkshire terriers. Gary knows what type he will get from putting a dog to a bitch and, while not all are world beaters, most are typey enough to compete well at shows and the vast majority are ready for entering to fox by the age of twelve months.

If one is going to use a particular strain in order to improve working ability and looks, then, if consistent improvements are made, then one must line breed back to that strain and keep the bloodlines running strong. My own terriers have quite a bit of Middleton strain blood in their breeding and they are typey and excellent workers, but that blood is easily lost if I just bred them with any nondescript terrier. Breeding back to related stock is the only way of breeding consistently good workers and lookers. Even then, one cannot guarantee top quality workers from every litter. Gary has bred a few that would not even look at a hole, even after giving them plenty of time to enter and allowing them to see other terriers at work. One of these was Basher, a white Lakeland that won many shows up and down the country after Gary had sold it because it would not enter. This dog ended up being bought by a Jack Russell enthusiast and was used to improve coat and general type in some Russell strains. I do not know if this dog eventually entered, but it certainly should have done, for it was bred from some of the best workers in the country and had every reason to take to its true vocation in life. A terrier that will not enter is usually mentally immature and is just not yet ready for the job. I have known some enter properly as late as their fourth or fifth year, so who knows, maybe Basher took to work in the end, but Gary could do nothing with the dog and this has been true of one or two others.

Gary keeps his terriers in prime condition and will not show them when they are freshly bitten. He allows the wounds to heal completely before he will even consider showing and treats bites regularly, keeping them clean and pulling off scabs that form, for this aids the healing process and it also means that scars are rarely permanent, for hair growth will soon cover old bite wounds when great care is taken to allow healing to occur in the best possible way. Gary has few problems anyway, with fresh bites during the showing season, for he packs up at the end of winter, or very early spring, strongly believing in a closed-season when foxes, unless taking lambs, should be left strictly alone. True, smooth coated terriers show scars far more easily, but harsh coated terriers will soon have scars covered and this, Gary believes, is the best way to exhibit, for he does not like to see badly scarred Lakelands in the ring. He is certainly not against scars, for he knows better than most that scars are picked up, especially by harder dogs, and he cites the case of Breay's Bingo. Bingo, being slape-coated (a dense smooth coat), carried many visible scars, but both Breay and Buck always made sure their terriers were healed up *before* showing them.

Gary also likes any terrier breed that is pleasing to the eye and he will put up blacks, Russells, or border terriers if they meet his standard for a worker, including being spannable, for some have huge chests and simply will not get up to a fox in most earths. He has seen some very good-looking black terriers and tells a tale of a mating that is undoubtedly responsible for quite a few typey black terriers around today. George Lothian, the father-in-law of the late John Nicholson, one time Huntsman of the Lunesdale foxhounds, owned a black bitch named Grip, which was bred by Cyril Breay and was, to quote Gary, 'bull terrier in type' and thus being a little too wide in the chest for Middleton's liking. Gary remembers this bitch, for he knew Lothian well, and states that she was very game indeed. She was mated by a black and tan pedigree Lakeland terrier and whelped two pups later on. George Lothian kept one back and the other, Hector, served at the Lunesdale, Badger being the dog Lothian kept. Both grew to be very typey terriers and both were also very good workers. Lothian exhibited Badger all over the Lake District and did well with him (Gary says that Badger was possibly the most typey black terrier he has ever seen), eventually selling him to Frank Buck at the Patterdale show. Buck then sold the terrier to Charlie Dickenson of West Yorkshire, who was also known as 'Charlie stick' because he made very good quality walking sticks, and he then used this terrier to breed some very good-looking blacks when he put Badger at stud. Gary believes that the typey blacks that gave rise to the famous Beano were a product of this mating, though rumours became rife that Buck's Black Davey had sired Hector and Badger, but this simply wasn't true, for Gary can remember the mating that took place (he docked the two pups for Lothian), as well as the Lakeland that sired these two earth dogs. True, a mating by a pedigree Lakeland would do far more harm than good these days, but this occurred a long time ago and the two typey terriers were no worse off and were excellent workers, as well as show winners.

Although Gary breeds many self-entering Lakelands that take to their work very quickly and perform as though they are veterans at the game from day one (I have bred one or two such terriers myself and have seen complete novices enter massive earths and find in them as though they have been working for years), he believes certain rules should be followed. For instance, many will want to go to fox very early on and these should be held back. Also, he does not believe in allowing a puppy to taste a carcass at the end of a dig. If one allows a young entry to go to a fox once it is dead, then when it goes to live quarry it will be more than a little confused when it discovers they do not lie still, but fight with great ferocity. So he believes in putting a youngster to live quarry, once it has seen an experienced colleague at work, usually towards the end of a dig. He will use a baying bitch and allow the youngster to creep up the side of the bitch, as long as she is good tempered of course and she will not savage the novice out of jealousy, and begin working its fox, or, in the old days, badger.

When entering a terrier of uncertain ancestry, Gary believes that it should work for at least two seasons before breeding from it, but he does not believe this is necessary when one knows the strain one breeds inside out. He believes that, after only a few digs, he can tell the abilities of his terriers simply because they are all related and display the same qualities, so he will breed off a dog or bitch once it has proven itself at finding, staying and killing foxes if it is a dog. If the bitch proves a hard baying type, working close to her quarry until it bolts, or is dug out, or, indeed, she kills foxes, as some do, then he will breed from her as soon as is possible. This, he believes, is important, for each generation are essential in keeping the bloodlines pure and he is well aware that a terrier could easily be lost to ground before he has a chance to breed from it. So, once entered, he will test his terriers for consistency over a few digs, sometimes many digs, and then he will breed from them if he so wishes, or he deems it necessary to continue the bloodlines. The importance of using good dogs as soon as possible was brought home to him one day when he almost lost one of his best dogs.

Old Rex mated Judy (his daughter), the black and tan part Welsh bitch, and produced, among others, a very typey and strong dog, also named Rex. While still young and before having been used at stud, Gary took Rex to a valley near Preston where he was hunting foxes with his companion, Freddie Hoyle. They found a hole situated on a massive bank and the soil was a little sandy around the entrance, which worried Gary a little, for he is cautious about putting terriers into sand holes and stresses the importance of being careful where one enters a terrier. Rex was put in and soon found his fox, which wasn't for bolting. As they dug in Gary's worst fears were realised, for the soil gave out to sand and it was difficult digging, for sand falls in and the sides of a dig are very unstable. After some time, they heard a thud and knew immediately that the hole had collapsed and Gary now feared for the life of his dog. Rex was a fox killer and had engaged his quarry, but the tangle had caused the hole to collapse. They dug vigorously and, while Freddie was inside, the sand collapsed on top of him, but, thankfully, Gary was quickly able to pull him out. They then cleared the loose stuff and uncovered Rex and his quarry. Both were still alive, but had suffered due to lack of air. Rex hadn't the room or the breath to finish his foe before being dug out. This taught Gary to be choosy where he put a terrier and of the importance of using a stud, or a good bitch, as soon as they have proven themselves game.

He has lost a few terriers over the years, but not many, one of these being a blue and fawn dog that he put into a rock hole in the Winster valley. He cannot remember the name of the terrier, for this was in the early days and he would have been a son, or a grandson of Rock, and believes he probably came upon a badger and met his end, for some of these Middleton strain dogs close with 'Brock' as they would a fox.

Mist, of good type due to Middleton blood.

Mist, winner of her class.

Beck, daughter of Mist; another winner.

Barry Wild with his very typey black and tan dog, improved using
Middleton blood. Barry's terriers are also excellent workers.

A middleton bred pup similar in type to Wilk's Rock, a result of line breeding over many years.

A daughter of Chad and Barry Wild's black bitch.

Basher, a looker, but wouldn't enter. Middleton is honest enough to admit when one of his terriers won't work, though non-workers are rare.

Rex, nearly lost at Preston (sire: old Rex. Dam: Judy (part Welsh).

Granddaughter Yasmin with Mist at a show.

Gary and friends digging a fox in the south Lakes.

A Bill Brightmore black owned by Seamus Irwin. Put to Rex, this terrier became the ancestor of plenty of smart black stuff.

Tim, similar in type to old Rex, his great grandsire.

Chapter Six

THE WHITE LAKELAND

Lakeland terriers have been producing white puppies for generations and several of these have served at the various fell packs. Fox terrier blood has undoubtedly brought about this coloration that has led to an almost separate breed which is known as the white Lakeland, though other white bodied terriers have also played a part in the creation of the modern fell, or Lakeland, terrier.

The Redesdale terrier, bred around the north-eastern districts of England, was a rough coated all-white terrier, similar in type to the terrier in Marshall's painting of Francis Dukinfield Astley and his harriers which was painted during the early part of the nineteenth century. Although this terrier is smooth coated, it is a fine representation of the type of terrier being used with northern packs of hounds at that time and some bull terrier blood, or early bulldog blood, is obvious when one studies this painting.

I believe that the Redesdale terrier played an important part in early fell terrier bloodlines and this all-white colouring is seen on some fell and Lakeland terriers to this day. Pedigree fox terriers certainly played a massive part in improving type and there were plenty of breeders of this type of terrier to be found in the fell country during the latter part of the nineteenth century, such as a Mr Williams of Barrow-in-Furness and the Master and Huntsmen of the Carlisle and District Otterhounds, who bred and worked some incredibly game and good looking fox terriers. The fact that fell and Lakeland terrier litters consistently produce fox terrier marked puppies is proof that this breed was used when the show craze hit during the latter part of the nineteenth century, in order to improve looks for the showring.

Miners from Devon and Cornwall began working in the Lake District from 1830 onwards and these would surely have taken terriers with them to the Lakes. Also, it seems reasonable to assume that these miners returned with a few of the fell bred terriers and that these entered into the bloodlines of the dogs that gave rise to the pedigree fox terrier. Fred Barker certainly sent fell terriers to the south of England and these he swapped for white bodied earth dogs that he used as outcross blood for his own strain of working terrier that eventually gave rise to the Middleton strain of Lakeland. Gary has always believed that fell terriers have played a part in creating the fox terrier, long before Fred Barker sent his fell types, some of which were bred out of 'Chowt-faced' Rock, to the Ilfracombe badger digging club members who used these dogs for outcross blood, possibly in order to improve coat and constitution, for Barker's strain produced harsh Irish terrier type jackets that shed the wet and kept out the cold, despite hunting some of the coldest and wettest regions in Britain. Middleton showed me an old photograph of two of these early fox terriers that, he believes, display more than a hint of fell terrier about them. I can only agree with him and I believe that, long before Barker swapped dogs with the Devonshire badger diggers, the terriers belonging to those southern miners who came to the lakes in 1830, played a large part in influencing fell strains and that fell types were taken south and these entered white bodied strains that gave rise to the pedigree fox terrier. True, these white bodied terriers so beloved by Parson Russell and others of his generation, were famed for standing back from their quarry and bolting it unharmed to hounds, but that wasn't always the case.

Jock and Tartar were two famous fox terriers that Parson Russell borrowed in order to use them as studs for his bitches and these terriers were incredibly fiery and were noted as fierce cat killers and bad fighters. Terriers with such dispositions, if a fox will not bolt, will often kill their quarry below and one wonders if fell terrier blood was responsible for these characteristics. True, most fell types are not aggressive with other dogs, but some are and always have been, especially if they become bored and do not see enough work. Heinemann, the famous Devonshire terrier enthusiast and foxhunter, recorded that he had problems with harder terriers and on one occasion he dug to a fox that had been 'put in' by hounds and soon uncovered his terrier which had remained mute throughout and had fast hold of its quarry, intent on killing it. A result of bull terrier blood? Possibly, but this may also indicate a strong influence of early fell terrier blood.

Through the miners that worked the Lakeland fells from 1830 onwards, as well as the terriers sent to Devonshire by Fred Barker, I am certain that fell blood was used on white bodied terriers, though this may also have resulted from another means. Parson Russell was well known for being kind and considerate to Gypsies and other travelling folk and one can be certain that, even though I strongly believe that Russell did indeed breed his own strain of fox terrier, he would have acquired some excellent terriers from these people who travelled up and down the country. It is my belief that these travelling folk took different types of terrier with them on their journeys and sold them to foxhunters and badger diggers along the way. And thus the hardy fell terrier may well have arrived in southern districts by this route and would undoubtedly have entered local strains in order to improve gameness and coat type. A good coat is essential for terriers working the Exmoor and Dartmoor districts and some suffered badly whilst working such regions. Even Heinemann had problems with bad weather affecting his terriers and he sometimes resorted to leaving terriers at certain farmhouses that could easily be reached should they be required when a fox was either marked to ground, or 'put in' by hounds. True, he ran many of his terriers with hounds and often came upon an earth being marked by his pack, with the terrier already below ground, in much the same manner as did the Parson, but the weather 'played havoc', as he put it, with his terriers and he felt it prudent to protect them from the elements as best he could. For these reasons, fell terrier blood, I am certain, was used on many strains of southern white bodied terriers, for a hardier breed of earth dog would be hard to come by, having been used in the mountainous districts of Cumberland for hundreds of years.

It was such blood that entered the fell strains during the latter part of the nineteenth century and it was such blood that continued to be used in order to improve type for the showring. Bowman's Lil was the foundation stone for the Wilkinson strain and she was a white Lakeland that was possibly bred down from the fox terriers worked at the Carlisle and District Otterhound kennels. Sid began breeding from Lil in 1924 when Bowman retired and gave him this bitch (though Eddie Pool says that Lil was bought from Yorkshire by Sid's father. Of course, this may have been a different Lil, as this was a common name throughout northern hunt countries at that time), the bloodlines eventually producing Nettle and Rock. Fred Barker had used blood from the Ilfracombe badger digging club (Fred dug badger using 'Chowt-faced' Rock and his offspring) as an outcross for his game strain of earth dog and thus white bodied terriers, though white bodied terriers with quite a bit of fell terrier influence, Gary believes, entered fell strains via this route also.

No wonder then that, when Gary put his old Rex to Floss, a red bitch belonging to Ken James which was also bred down from Wilk's Rock and carried several lines to what Gary describes as 'the old Patterdale strain', two white Lakelands resulted. These were Gravel and Flint and Middleton kept Gravel, while Flint was sold to the Midlands where he founded a dynasty of top working and winning Jack Russell types. I once entered one of Flint's descendants for a friend and she had won thirteen show championships before she was twelve months of age, so one can easily imagine how typey some of these terriers are. Gravel became a famous working white Lakeland who, among others, produced Billy, one of the smartest of all white Lakelands, described by Gary as being 'like an old fashioned fox terrier in type', and a hooligan of a dog that would kill any fox he could get his teeth into and who was far too hard for use at badger, though Gary dug quite a few using this terrier. Like old Rex, his grandsire, Billy was completely mute and Gary had to dig to the bumpings and bangings going on underground as the combatants tangled with one another. Middleton dug with him up and down the country and also in Ireland. He dug quite a number of foxes with this terrier at Winster, Brigsteer and other places throughout south Cumbria, as well as in West Yorkshire where Gary has done much of his hunting. Gravel was put to a bitch called Becky, a white Lakeland owned by Peter Maguire of Wigan, and it was this union that produced Billy and his brother which was given a rather curious nick-name. Billy's brother was almost all-white, with two large brown rings around both eyes which earned him the honour of being known as 'Roy Orbison'. This terrier, like many of Middleton's stock, had the characteristic ''ead like a brick' and he made quite a name for himself around the Lancashire area where he was used for digging plenty of stuff. As Gary put it, 'he was a 'ell of a dog'.

There were quite a few digging lads around the Wigan area at this time and I remember some of them very well indeed. They didn't breed any particular strain of terrier, but used a variety, including Buck/Breay stuff, Middleton strain Lakelands, Cowan strain Lakelands, or anything else that would work, for they were serious digging lads and took large hauls of foxes and badgers throughout Lancashire and beyond. They had some superb workers and I saw a few of them at fox and was most impressed.

By his fifth season, Billy had lost most of his teeth in skirmishes with foxes and badgers and Gary was forced to retire him. He headed to the south of England and became a famous stud dog, siring top winning Russell types, true, but also producing incredibly game workers that are being used by digging lads throughout Kent and other districts not far from London. In fact, there are a surprising number of digging lads in these areas who are using middleton strain Lakelands for fox bolting and digging.

Before he headed south, however, Billy had already sired a dynasty of terriers and his offspring are being worked and shown up and down the country, as well as in Ireland, Canada and America. Ruth, Gary's wife, remembers Billy well as she attempted to make a 'house dog' of him. She remarked, quite dryly, that Billy was rather strong willed, even as a young puppy, and quickly showed his instinct for work, though not quite in the conventional way. One day Ruth had let him out and he decided he would like to attack and kill the ducks that were out on the frozen pond. However, out towards the middle the ice was thinner and Billy broke through it, falling into the icy water. Ruth heard him barking, but thought he was maybe trying to dig up a mouse or something.

Eventually, however, she went to investigate and saw him trapped in the middle of the pond. She confesses that she thought, only for a second or so, of leaving him there, he was that much of a nuisance, but couldn't bring herself to do such a thing. In the end she went inside for her wellies and walked out to fetch him. The only trouble was, she forgot just how deep the pond was and the four feet of ice-cold water was soon over the tops of her boots. Billy was in a bad way and was probably moments from death when Ruth rescued him, so she put him in front of the fire and knew within an hour that he was back to his old self again, for he tried worrying the cat!

Ruth owned a very smart border terrier called Ben, a dog she enjoyed considerable success with in the showring, including kennel club shows, and Billy suddenly rounded on him and attacked him while Gary's mum and the family were enjoying tea on the lawn. After much screaming at him and with a joint effort, they managed to get Billy off Ben and things soon settled down, though Gary's mum told Ruth to get her a lead and she would take him to the vet and have him put down immediately. It was shortly after this that Billy was put into the kennel, for Ruth's nerves were far too frayed to put up with him around the house any longer.

Of course all of this was an indication that Billy had a very strong working instinct and he certainly proved it when Gary entered him. He killed many foxes during his working life and was used on quite a number of badgers too. When Gary was in Ireland, Billy was put into an earth that has quite a reputation as a bad place. Gary would only enter Billy to badgers if the earth was shallow and easily dug, for a long dig would see the terrier possibly killed, or very seriously injured at best, so he was a little worried when his terrier found a badger in the earth, rather than a fox. After quite a hard dig, Gary dug to Billy and he had bottled up two badgers, but, as you can imagine, because of his disposition, had taken quite a mauling as a result. Like Rex, Billy never learned to avoid injury when at badger and he never quite had the knack his grandsire had of totally dominating his foe until the badger turned away, unwilling to face its opponent any longer. However, Billy was a very useful worker and as a terrier for carrying out serious fox control in earths that were virtually impossible to dig, he was unbeatable.

Billy became famous for other reasons too. Mainly because he has sired some incredibly good looking Jack Russell types that are winning well throughout the country. Also, the Parson Jack Russell owes much of its type to Billy, for he was used extensively by some top Russell breeders to put the coat and general type back into what is considered to be the parson's ideal working terrier. Top winning Russells throughout Britain, Ireland and America owe much of their type to Billy and his offspring and, though Gary will not name names for obvious reasons, he has had many breeders use this terrier, or his sons, in order to get the type of Russell they require. In fact, I have known some breeders use coloured terriers too, from Middleton's strain, which have been resorted to because many of the old 'Russell' types were bandy legged and with poor coats and general type.

As Gary stated, Billy and his progeny are of the old fashioned fox terrier in type and Russell breeders just couldn't resist using such blood. And why not. Personally, I do not think there is anything wrong with this, for, after all, white Lakelands are descended from old fashioned fox terriers of the type the Parson favoured. The only problem with resorting to such blood is that the progeny are often too hard and will not stand off and bay at their quarry, but will close with it and kill it instead. For those who admire a traditional Jack Russell for its 'gentler' qualities while at work, the white Lakeland influence isn't at all favoured.

Bob and Ruth Arnold of Kent have been breeding, showing and working Middleton bred Lakelands for many years now and their foundation stone was Sid Wilkinson's Jock, a son of the inevitable Rock, which was with Bill Brightmore who became a good friend of the Arnold's. Ruth can remember Jock as an old dog, aged fourteen, being taken out of his box and fed by Bill, who remarked that the old lad was lining a bitch that afternoon! She isn't sure whether he was serious or not, but she can well believe it, for Jock sired many litters of Lakeland terrier over the years, even into old age, he had such a reputation as a worker, though he was quite a looker too. Jock saw the latter years of Sid Wilkinson and became too much for the old gentleman who could no longer keep him occupied with plenty of work, which his sire had enjoyed, and would bite Sid's legs when he was attempting to exhibit him, so he was passed to Bill who worked him and used him to serve many bitches. The North Pennines, where Bill often hunted and where, incidentally, Fred

Barker often used 'Chowt-faced' Rock for fox hunting and badger digging, holds several bad earths that cannot possibly be dug and so Jock was used to kill any foxes that would not bolt from such places, sometimes being used with the Lunesdale foxhounds, or the Ullswater pack.

Like many of this strain, Jock produced the odd white puppy in his litters and these were so typey and were so close to the 'fourteen inch, fourteen pound' standard for Jack Russells that a dynasty of Lakeland bred whites has sprung up from the original Lakeland terrier bloodlines. Bob and Ruth Arnold have bred some very good white Lakelands too and they have won well at shows over the years, with both coloureds and whites. Ruth has won, among many others, best Lakeland twice at the Great Yorkshire show, she has won the Midland Game Fair and champion pup twice at Lowther, the home show, if you like, of the Lakeland terrier. And, what is best of all, every terrier shown in adult classes by Bob and Ruth Arnold has been tested as to working ability first. Bob cannot engage in digs as often as he used to do, but he has family who work his terriers whenever he is unable and all are entered when he deems them ready.

I asked Ruth why Bob and herself have chosen to stick with the Middleton strain of terrier. For Ruth, it is the consistency of good looking types that attracts her, for she is very keen on exhibiting, and she remarked that some of the same qualities are displayed with each successive generation. She admires the way the dog terriers are so cocky and so full of themselves, always being alert, keen and workmanlike, and she says that they often begin cocking their legs by the age of twelve weeks, which is a very unusual peculiarity, but a trait that may help to explain why many Middleton bred terriers, particularly dog terriers, are ready to enter at a far younger age than many other strains. Bob has entered some of his terriers as early as ten months and they have killed foxes at such a 'tender' age. They obviously mature very quickly, for Gary has known six month old pups enter to fox, though he strongly advises against entering at such a young age.

For Bob, it is the consistency with which good workers are produced throughout each generation. True, not every Middleton strain terrier will make an exceptional worker, and a very small number may even be poor workers. Gary is honest enough to admit that he has occasionally bred a terrier that just will not enter, while others have been average workers, but the majority, at least 75%, make good workers, while quite a large percentage go on to become exceptional workers if given the chance. Many exceptional workers have been produced over the years and the names of some of these easily trip off Middleton's tongue. Rex, of course, was one of his best and the hardest terrier he has ever seen at work.

Tim was another very good worker and he was quite a typey son of Wilk's Rock. Tiny was one of his best and she was an early bitch, which carried quite a bit of the Dent strain in her line. He has bred at least two exceptional Jocks and Nailer, the son of the first Jock, was another excellent worker which had no reverse gears whatsoever. Nettle, the bitch with which Gary dug five badger in one day, was another cracker, as was Trixie, the red bitch and the mother to Jewel, another superb working bitch which closely resembled Rock, her grandsire, and was as hard as a dog at her work. Some of the later terriers were Toby, the terrier that sired Tyke and Twist, Rocky, a hard fox killer with a superb head, and white-footed Rocky, another exceptional earth dog. I could go on and on with this list, for there have been countless terriers called Rex, Rusty, Punch, Trouble, Rock, Rags, that have been very good at their work.

Gary states that quite a lot of folk put his dogs onto their bitches and that they then breed from someone else's dog of another strain and so eventually lose the blood of his strain. But when that strain produces a non-worker, he often takes the blame and his family of terriers is then credited with being a non-working strain, being show dogs only. His 'pure' strain continues to produce very good and useful workers and many digging lads are either using dogs bought direct from Gary, or they have brought his blood into their own strains in order to produce more determined workers and to improve type also. As Barry Wild once said, Middleton has succeeded in capturing the bloodlines of the best workers in the Lake District and this makes it easier for breeders today, if they wish to bring this blood into their own strains. Gary states that they must then line breed in order to keep that blood and use more of his stud dogs if they are to truly benefit. In fact, if one wishes to improve the looks and ability of one's strain, then you could do no better than imitate Gary Middleton when he was intent on improving his Dent strain of terrier by using Wilk's Rock, sons and grandsons of Rock, as much as possible. If one puts a Middleton stud onto the best bitch in the kennel, and then a bitch pup is put to Joe Bloggs dog of no particular breeding, and then Fred Smith has a good dog that is someone else's breeding and another bitch is put to that, and indifferent workers result, then it can hardly be claimed that Middleton's stuff did nothing to improve a strain of working terrier. There have only been a few generations since Wilk's Rock and the blood of those early exceptional workers still runs strong to this day and crops up in the modern strain on a fairly regular basis, so the use of Middleton blood to improve a strain, and then going back to more Middleton blood to reinforce the bloodlines, will only benefit a strain of terrier that needs improving.

Bob and Ruth Arnold breed the 'pure' Middleton lines and they have had a number of dogs from Gary himself. The exceptionally hard white Lakeland, Billy, ended his days at Ruth's kennels and she bred, among others, a superb worker named Jed out of this dog, when he was put to Nut, a terrier Gary gave her. Jed entered well to fox and was fully tested before going to America for racoon hunting, where this terrier acquitted itself well, though it eventually died whilst at its work.

Rocky went down to Ruth's kennels in Kent and he too was a famous worker and show winner with that characteristic large head of a type similar to Sid's old dog. Ruth also had Judy from Gary, a later bitch and a daughter of Rocky, which was loaned to me for some time before she headed south. I found Judy to be of excellent temperament and she came to me as an unentered bitch, though she took to the game very easily and was particularly useful for mink hunting. I enjoyed some superb mink hunts with this bitch and she was very keen indeed and possessed a very good nose for marking, despite her inexperience. Punch was another terrier I worked with which headed south and he came a little bit later than Judy. Punch was very typey and another easily entered terrier, but if he had a fault it was his back legs, which were a little unsightly.

For those who admire a baying sort of Jack Russell, then the white Lakeland is best avoided, for many are very game and prove too hard for fox bolting to hounds. Even some of the bitches prove too hard and they are almost suicidal in their approach to their work. One of these was a white bitch that Gary recently sold to Ireland. She was keen to enter and so Gary took her out for the first time when she was just twelve months of age. She was quite a looker and had already been offered good money for her, but Gary was reluctant to part with her just yet, especially as she hadn't been tried at fox. At Keighley, near an old factory where new building work was going on, Gary and his companions had a look round the site and found quite a shallow hole freshly dug into a bank of soil recently moved by a digger. They didn't think there would be anything in this earth, but the bitch was keen and so Middleton gave her a chance. She entered the place and, indeed, there was a fox at home. The bitch then proceeded to finish her quarry below ground, and very quickly, and she then drew the carcass out of the hole. This was a very good start to a promising career and, after Gary had taken quite a few foxes with her and had enjoyed success in the showring too, he sold her to Ireland, but warned the buyer to keep her out of places where badgers may be lurking, for she was so hard that she was sure to come unstuck at such quarry.

However, the reader knows as well as I do that it is utterly impossible to know if a badger has popped into a fox earth for the day, for whatever reason, and avoiding them 100% just cannot be predicted. True, it is easy to identify a badger sett and thus such places are avoided by law-abiding terriermen, but occasionally a badger may be found lurking in a fox earth without there being any sign of such occupation. This happened in Ireland. The new owner, impressed with this bitch and her ability to finish foxes, entered her into a drain and she quickly engaged her quarry. They found the antagonists half a field away and dug down, only to find the bitch had been killed by 'Brock'. She had tackled it head on, as she would a fox, and had died as a result. Gary was 'sick' when he heard the news, for she was an exceptionally game and typey bitch, which could be traced all the way back to Rex, through Billy and Gravel. Her bloodlines were important to Middleton's breeding programme, but, obviously, they are no longer available, though he can continue breeding through other related stock.

Soda was another superb terrier of the white Lakeland type and he was a son of Billy who won certificates for traditional earthwork in Ireland. Soda, like his sire, had a terrific head and he could finish any fox that would not bolt. Gary dug plenty of stuff using this dog and there are many witnesses who can verify the abilities of Soda and other white Lakelands.

There are a number of breeders of Jack Russells who have stayed clear of the white Lakeland influence and they have successfully bred some good types, but the old fashioned fox terrier type, generally speaking, has been brought about with the use of white Lakeland blood, particularly white Lakelands from the Middleton strain of working terrier.

Billy as a puppy.

Billy as an adult (ph. Bob and Ruth Arnold).

Jed, out of Billy and Nut. Jed went to America working racoons (ph. Bob and Ruth Arnold).

Gin at Patterdale show. She was later stolen.

A terrier out of Billy at Lowther.

Pippa, out of coloured parents Jessie and Punch – the same who worked with hill pack in Wales.

A white out of a coloured litter.

Frost, out of Billy and Nut (ph. Bob and Ruth Arnold).

The white bitch entered at Keighley and killed by badger in Ireland.

Old fashioned fox terriers similar in type to today's white Lakelands.

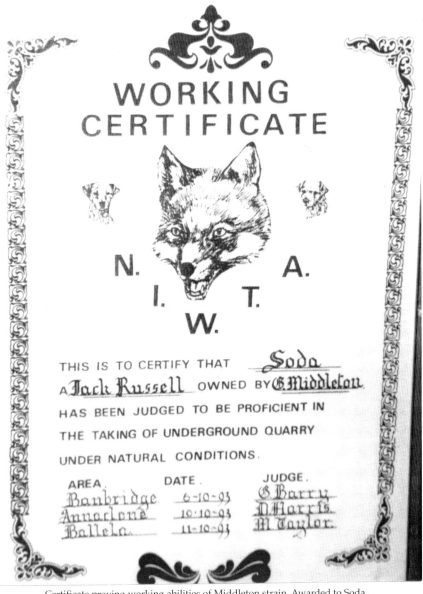

WORKING
CERTIFICATE

N.
I.
W.
A.
T.

THIS IS TO CERTIFY THAT _Soda_

A **Jack Russell** OWNED BY **G Middleton**

HAS BEEN JUDGED TO BE PROFICIENT IN
THE TAKING OF UNDERGROUND QUARRY
UNDER NATURAL CONDITIONS.

AREA	DATE	JUDGE
Banbridge	6-10-93	G Barry
Annaclone	10-10-93	D Harris
Ballela	11-10-93	M Taylor

Certificate proving working abilities of Middleton strain. Awarded to Soda.

IV·EAGH
TERRIER CLUB

Certificate
of Merit

This is to certify that

Soda, a Jack Russell Terrier

the property of Garry Middleton

at major trials held on Sept,12ᵗʰ 1993 *.*

at Banbridge, Co.Down, N.L.

satisfied the Judges in every respect

Denis Harris.........

John Barry.........

Michael Taylor...

A second certificate awarded to Soda.
These were for digs held on 12/9/93, 6/10/93, 10/10/93 and 11/10/93 in different locations.

A red Lakeland with white blaze, betraying fox terrier ancestry.

MR. FRANCIS DUKINFIELD ASTLEY AND HIS HARRIERS

Astley's terrier of a type similar to the Redesdale and some early fox terriers (early 19th century).

137

Chapter Seven

REMINISCENCES OF GAME TERRIERS

Mac was one of Middleton's early terriers and Sheila Barker remembers this dog well, for he had no reverse gears and took terrific punishment when tackling 'Brock', rather than give ground, and she helped treat the terrier on these occasions, for Gary dug fox and badger with Anthony Barker and Sid Wilkinson almost every Sunday at this time. Mac could draw a badger out from under immovable rocks and he was known to kill foxes if they would not bolt, for he was tremendously hard and allowed few to escape.

Gary had arranged to go digging with Ken Simpson, but he had overslept and Ken threw stones up at the window in order to rouse Middleton from slumber, telling him that something was going on in his back garden. Gary had recently purchased a large sow and Mac had somehow escaped from his kennel and had attacked the unfortunate pig. By the time Gary reached the antagonists, the pig was in its final struggle against impending death and Mac was badly injured, his front leg severely bitten. Mac would not give in and eventually won the contest and this had been yet another demonstration of how game this terrier was. Gary admired such game qualities and bred frequently from this dog, producing some typey black and tan and red offspring that, like their sire, were excellent workers. Mac was so game that even Anthony Barker showered praise on the dog, after he had seen him draw a 'Brock' from under a massive rock close to the shores of Ullswater lake.

Middleton had another dog of the same name, but much later, a terrier sired by a black and tan dog called Rex (Gary has had several terriers with this name). He was out near Huddersfield with Barry Kay and they were checking an earth on the bank of an old railway line, an earth full of cinders which can make digging rather difficult. Mac was a red dog and this was his first outing. He sniffed at the entrance and was certainly keen, so Gary loosed him and allowed him a try. Mac entered and quickly found his fox, drawing it out of the earth and finishing it off as he did so. The fox had fastened its teeth through his foot and he had drawn it without letting go, or even flinching.

Tim was another son of Rock and he was incredibly game indeed and was used extensively to continue Middleton's breeding programme. A rather unusual event occurred while Tim was still a pup and with his litter mates. Gary had allowed them out into the sun for a while and the litter were playing, or mouching around in the grass, when a buzzard suddenly flew in and picked up one of the pups, taking it onto the shed roof and killing it there, though Gary tried his hardest to get the bird to release the pup before it was killed. His efforts failed and the bird flew off with its prize. Tim went on to be yet another hard fox killing terrier and he saw plenty of service with both hounds and on private digs.

The black and tan dog, Rags, was a son of old Rex and, like his sire, had proven incredibly game. He had seen service down in Wales in the Ynsfor Hunt country, taking part in many badger digs and had so impressed major Roche that he had bought terriers from Gary since that time. Gary says that Major Roche toured the Lake District once a year and bought and took back with him a few of the gamer Lakeland terriers that he could purchase, which rather puts in doubt the theory that the Ynsfor bred and used their own strain of black and tan terrier bred out of the foundation terriers of the Welsh. This may have been true, but what is certain is that many Lakeland bred terriers, including those belonging to Middleton, returned to Wales with the major, and his friend Mr Williams, and that these were then used with the Ynsfor pack.

Rags had seen service down in Wales and had acquitted himself well, but one of the most memorable hunts with this dog was in the Winster valley, not far from Gary's home. Rags was a very strong terrier with the characteristic massive head and had proven useful at both fox and badger. Gary was hunting with Malcolm Lambert at the time and Rags was entered into a large rock earth that is well known as quite a bad place, for it is utterly undiggable. Middleton thought a fox was at home, for Rags was keen and entered like wildfire, but it soon became obvious that this was no fox.

Some time later, and after Rags had tangled with his foe, a badger bolted from under a big rock and ran off unharmed, and then another suddenly appeared, but seemed to be stuck fast, for it wasn't moving any further. In actual fact, Rags had hold of its backside and eventually after much tugging, he began pulling 'Brock' back inside the den. There was little Gary could do, for the badger's head was free to inflict injury if he went too near, and so they watched as the badger disappeared back under the rock. Rags must have then released his hold, probably in order to get a better purchase, or maybe because 'Billy' had found some room and had turned around to defend itself, and that is when the second badger bolted and made off across the fell. Gary stated that, when digging to Rags, it was unusual to have to dig right to the stop-end where he had bottled up his quarry, whether it be fox or badger, for he would draw it out as Gary got ever closer to him, though, of course, it was usually a fox carcass that he pulled out, rather than live quarry! Rags drew many badgers throughout his career and, again, he was used quite a bit to continue such game bloodlines. Rags was sired by Rex and was out of Nettle, a game bitch sired by Tim, the other son of Rock, so he was closely related to Sid Wilkinson's old dog.

This account reminds me of another incident that occurred when John, mentioned earlier, was out with his Middleton bred terriers. He was hunting high ground and came upon a three-holed earth on top of a moor. Flint, one of his best dogs, was keen to go and so he was loosed. This was a typical fox earth, not too deep and with enough bolt holes to allow the quarry to flee quickly, and he waited outside with his lurcher, while the terrier explored the dark passages underground, searching for his elusive quarry. It wasn't long before Flint began baying and John was certain a fox would soon be out, but the terrier settled in one spot and continued to bark at his foe, which was a little unusual, for he expected his dog to tackle his fox, rather than bay at it.

However, a little later, things started to move and suddenly a large badger bolted from the earth. John held onto his lurcher, of course, and allowed 'Billy' to escape unharmed, but was then quickly over to the earth in order to grab his earth dog, lest it chase after its foe and get into a deeper sett. Flint showed his face at the exit, but then quickly returned and John then knew another was at home. Sure enough, Flint began baying again and soon after the second badger, another large specimen, bolted and made off. Flint only had a few bites, for he had avoided tackling it as he would a fox, and John was able to get hold of him as he emerged.

Gary has seen some excellent working terriers up and down the country and these have represented all of the working terrier breeds, from Jack Russells, to borders, to black terriers (he will not call black terriers Patterdales, for he is adamant that this name fits the type of terrier he breeds, for he has never seen this type, the type beloved by Breay and Buck, bred anywhere near the Patterdale area) to bedlingtons, and a host of other breeds. He admires such terriers and those who work them, but he cannot stand the chap who stands at the bar, a pint in his fist, who goes on about how much his dogs can do, when everybody knows he rarely, if ever, works his terriers.

He has known a few such terrier breeders over the years and has often listened to their boasting at terrier shows inside the inevitable beer tent. At a show at Lorton, inside the Melbreak country, Gary was tired of hearing such boastings from a small group who were known to rarely work their terriers, yet they paraded them at shows all over the Lakes. So, in the end, he challenged them. There was a large sett, in fact, it is still there to this day, on the hillside far above the showground and it could be seen from where they stood at the entrance to the beer tent. Middleton then suggested that they all get their terriers together at an appointed date and dig that sett, in order to see who had the gamest workers. He had no takers and the boasting ended abruptly for that day!

Gary was once on a badger dig at Patterdale and had already started, when Anthony Barker and Charlie 'stick' duly arrived and got stuck into the proceedings. Charlie was a good friend of Barker's and often stayed at his farm on the outskirts of Patterdale, enjoying hunts with the Ullswater foxhounds, as well as taking part in the private Sunday digs that became famous around the Ullswater district. Middleton had Judy to ground that day and she had already made quite a name for herself working both foxes and badgers, for it was the same bitch who had drawn those thirty foxes out from under that shed at Crook. Judy was so game that, rather than give an inch, she sometimes took fearful maulings instead, especially when at badger, losing an ear and part of her nose during this particular dig.

Charlie, like many fell hunters, admired a game terrier and he offered Gary twenty-five pounds for his bitch, saying, "yer might as well tek it, she might die anyroad, state she's in." This sum of money was ridiculously high in those early days, even for an entered terrier, which tells us something of the abilities of this bitch. Gary had already been offered decent money for his Lakeland, especially after drawing those foxes, but had refused as she was so important to Middleton's breeding programme. However, he had bred a number of litters from her by now and had a few youngsters to bring on, so he summed up the situation and sold her. Judy, of course, didn't die and was soon back to working condition. She headed to Yorkshire and undoubtedly bred some game stock and her descendants will no doubt still be found around the Pennine districts of Lancashire and Yorkshire. This Judy was not the daughter of old Rex and the black and tan terrier from Wales, though this bitch was utterly game too, but a bitch bred out of Rock, one of the pair of terriers returned to Sid Wilkinson after they had been sold as pets and had become too much for their new owner, frustrated at not being given access to work. Johnny Richardson's strain could be found in the bloodlines of Rock, but he was mostly bred out of Sid's old stuff, through old Rock himself. These two terriers were typey and won well at shows, but they were even better workers and settled somewhat, now that they were allowed to exercise their working instincts.

Middleton has travelled over to Ireland on numerous occasions and has taken part in a lot of digs over on the Emerald Isle and one of his best friends over there is Seamus Irwin; a chap who has a canny knack of catching foxes and who works as a professional pest control officer. He mainly uses his gun, lamping foxes at night and shooting them, or he takes them with lurchers, but one of his best methods is to use his 'quarter to three' dog!

A strange name and one, I think, that beats all of the unusual terrier names that come out of the Lake District, but a name that is rather apt, I suppose! Seamus named him such because all four legs are bandy and turn out at the paws, like the hands of a clock pointing to quarter to three. An amusing way of naming a dog, true, but there is nothing amusing in the way this dog works and Seamus has taken literally hundreds of foxes using this terrier. He is, I suppose, what one would describe as a Jack Russell, though, obviously, he is not typical of the type the Parson favoured, though he would undoubtedly be pleased with the abilities of this dog.

'Quarter to three' dog completely ignores badgers and is thus the perfect terrier for use at fox by a pest controller, for he will simply pass a badger by if one is found lurking in an earth, in order to get to his fox. He will then bolt the fox and Seamus will shoot it, for he is an expert shot. He will simply walk a hedge and allow his terrier to check the earths. The dog will sniff at each entrance and walk on if an earth is empty, but if he goes to ground, then Seamus knows that a fox is at home and will get his gun ready for imminent action. Gary has known Seamus take thirty and forty foxes in a week using this terrier and he was working that many that it got to the stage where it was becoming impossible to keep the dog working, he was getting bitten that many times.

Seamus then came up with an ingenius plan and Gary says that, if he hadn't seen this for himself, he simply wouldn't have believed it. He made a metal mask for 'Quarter to three' dog that fit snugly to his head, with a plate over his muzzle, which would prevent many strikes from reaching home. Seamus' plan worked. The terrier was in full swing again, but Gary remarked that the mask was full of dents and scratches, where Reynard had tried to strike at the baying terrier, before finally bolting. "It is the only way I can keep him going." Seamus remarked to Gary, as Middleton stood there looking at the unusual sight of the bandy-legged earth dog attired in his protective armour. And one can easily imagine this to be true, for a dog required to work between thirty and forty foxes a week, is sure to suffer many bites, even if it is of the baying type.

Gary remarked that his strain of terrier would not suit Seamus, for he needs a dog that will go in, bark at, tease, nip, and generally annoy, its fox, until it flees the earth and can be taken above ground. Seamus has taken part in many long and gruelling digs and he is a much-respected terrierman, but his job is controlling pests and he takes that many foxes that he simply cannot waste too much time digging, so he requires a fox to be bolted as quickly as possible. He keeps Russell types in the main, for Middleton's strain would allow few to bolt for him, especially the harder dog terriers. Gary stated that, if the 'Quarter to three' dog wagged its tail, even slightly, before entering an earth, then Seamus would know they were onto a fox. This type of terrier is ideal for Seamus' job, but would not suit what Middleton requires of a terrier. It is a case of 'each to his own' and what suits one terrierman, will not suit another.

Gary, Seamus and one or two other friends, once took part in a gruelling thirteen foot dig in Ireland and one of Seamus Irwin's Russell types was used throughout this dig, though Middleton had a young dog he was just starting called Jack, who was fourteen months of age at the time and he was a white Lakeland bred down from the Gravel, Billy bloodlines. They eventually broke through after digging out a massive trench (see photograph) and Jack was tried towards the end of the dig. Reynard was in a bit of an awkward spot, just around the corner of a tight passage from where he could inflict damage on an inexperienced young entry. Jack, however, was keen to go and Middleton loosed him. He went around the corner, took a bite or two from his new found foe, and then erupted, taking hold of his fox and killing it extremely quickly. Middleton was offered money for Jack before he returned to England, the lads were so impressed with how quickly and eagerly this dog had entered.

Gary has dug plenty of stuff throughout Scotland and was once hunting up in the Highlands with a pack of Sealyham type terriers that were used to hunt whin bushes (a northern name for gorse), flushing foxes to waiting guns. As they were waiting and watching closeby, they saw something run across the ground and enter an earth on the bank. They were not too sure of what they had seen, for it was simply a brown streak moving swiftly, so

Seamus Irwin and Gary Middleton at a show.

Gary and Seamus standing in the 13ft trench where Jack entered to his first fox.

George Norman; was present when old Rex finished two foxes during a dig in Scotland.

This typey red terrier is now at work in Scotland, after entering to its first fox.

Gary with his current stud dog Rex, a breeder of excellent working and good looking Lakelands.

they went over and Gary entered one of his terriers. He cannot remember which, for this was in the early days, though it may have been Rex, Tim, or possibly Chip, or even one of the harder bitches such as Trixie, Jewel, or Judy. A battle-royal took place and they dug to a depth of around three feet, when they uncovered the terrier and a now very dead Scottish Wildcat, the head of which Gary has mounted on his wall. Scottish Wildcats are extremely game fighters (as the terrier could have testified) and any terrier that will face one is considered very game indeed by the Scots. In fact, this was the test card for any earth dog of the Scottish breeds during earlier decades and any that would not kill a fully grown wildcat, were not considered game enough to perpetuate a strain.

Rags, the red bitch that Gary took to Wales alongside Rags, the black and tan dog, was another extremely game terrier and was not a baying type, for she would kill foxes and tackle badgers almost as hard, which meant that she sometimes suffered quite badly. After one particularly hard dig in the Lakes, Gary recovered his bitch and her quarry and she had taken quite a mauling, with one of her front legs badly broken. The vet wanted to amputate, but Gary refused, for he knew it would mean the end of her career, so he went to see a friend of his in Kendal; a doctor who was rather meticulous in his care of patients. Middleton waited until after surgery hours and then took the bitch to see him. This doctor was a countryman and knew all about working terriers and hunting in the Lakes and he had a look at the leg, deeming it very badly smashed, but, hopefully, repairable.

He set to immediately and put the bitch out, cleaning the wound and starting to operate there and then. He took off three of her toes, which could not be saved, and then skillfully pinned the bone together. All that was left was to wait patiently and this Gary did. He stated that the bone knit perfectly and she was soon sound again, though he said that her leg never quite put on as much muscle as before, so, if one looked carefully, one could just detect that this leg was a little thinner than the other. Of course, once the hair had grown back, it was hard to see anything unusual, even though three of her toes were missing.

One of Gary's earlier terriers was a bitch called Jet. She was very game and very vociferous, unlike some, which were mute while at work. Gary put her in an earth at Winster, but there was no sound, which was rather unusual, for this bitch made plenty of noise at her work and was much easier to dig down to because of this. Rex and Billy, among others, compelled Gary to dig down to bumps and grunts in the main, for they made little noise, preferring to seize their quarry, rather than bay at it, but terriers like Jet enabled the going to be far easier as all of the noise guided the diggers, but not on this occasion. Middleton dug down to where he thought the bitch was and came upon a wasps nest, and his bitch, who was in rather a bad state, for the wasps were all over her; in her ears, up her nose, and stinging any part of her anatomy they could reach, for the dense fur protected her in places. He managed to get her out, after receiving several stings himself, and it took her quite some time to recover. In fact, Gary says, she nearly died and probably would have done, had not her fur given her some protection from that angry swarm.

Danny Sykes had a similar incident with one of his terriers and a similar thing happened to myself a couple of years ago. I was out walking my small pack of terriers, when they began marking at a hole on the bank of a fishing pond. Thinking they had found a rat, or possibly a mink, I headed over to them, just in time to see a swarm of wasps erupting from that hole and attacking the dogs, as well as myself. I ran for all I was worth and was chased (and stung) for quite some distance, before I finally managed to evade them. The dogs had fared a lot better than myself, for they have dense fur which prevented many stings from making contact, but I had well over a dozen stings and felt rather unwell for days afterwards.

One of the best terriers Gary owned was a black and tan dog named Rusty (Middleton doesn't allow mere detail to get in the way when he is naming his dogs) who was a son of old Rex and a very game dog, like his famous sire. A friend of his telephoned him one day, asking if he could loan out one of his terriers, preferably a fox killing type, as he was a gamekeeper and was having problems with fox predation. Gary, being a generous sort, agreed, loaning Rusty for a couple of months. As time went by, Middleton enquired about the terrier, for the two months had long since passed by, but the chap said that he needed Rusty for a little longer.

It was some time after this that Gary went to the Bramham Moor Hunt show and, typically, he did rather well that day. The Huntsman then invited Gary to have a look at the hunt terriers, as they had acquired a superb dog that was quite a looker and an even better worker, and all the bitches were being lined by this dog. Middleton was rather surprised to find Rusty in kennel, but he didn't let on at first. He asked from where they had acquired the terrier and the Huntsman, after boasting about how good a worker Rusty was and saying that he had lined a few of their bitches, explained that a gamekeeper had loaned it to them and this turned out to be the chap to whom Gary had loaned Rusty months before. Middleton then explained the situation and, of course, the Huntsman returned the terrier to its rightful owner. When Gary arrived back home, he telephoned the keeper and asked how the terrier was doing. "Oh, he's doin' fine, a reyt good job, but ah need him a little bit longer." Came the sheepish reply. Middleton then informed him that he had been to the kennels and had picked up his terrier. That rogue of a keeper had been loaning the dog out for use at fox and for breeding purposes and was obviously pocketing the stud fees! Still, Gary is a forgiving sort of chap and remained friends with him for many years afterwards.

To say that Middleton has been a wild man, particularly in his younger days, is, I feel, rather an understatement, and, as one can imagine, Ruth has often had to put on the role of 'long-suffering wife.' She recalls a time, many years ago when they lived in their cottage at Crook, when Gary returned home with two new lurchers. Middleton has owned some cracking fox-catching lurchers over the years and only recently lost a bedlington cross which, despite its small size, was a game foxing dog. He installed these in their newly refurbished kitchen and left them there overnight. When Ruth came down in the morning, there was dog muck everywhere and much of the kitchen furniture was chewed up and completely ruined. As you can imagine, Ruth was not happy at all and other arrangements were made for the two running dogs.

On another occasion Gary headed off to Kendal for some paint and never returned. He was out all night and didn't come home the next morning, so Ruth telephoned the police. The officer on the other end of the line simply stated, "oh, he'll turn up." Eventually Gary did indeed 'turn up' and he had gone to Bill Brightmore's where he had been digging around Brough and Appleby. Ruth said that Gary did this regularly and would often just disappear, usually heading over to Patterdale where he would go digging with Sid Wilkinson and Anthony Barker. Ruth has known him go to Patterdale on a Monday and not return until the Thursday, having spent the week digging foxes and badgers and celebrating the hunts at local hostelries. There is no doubt that Gary was a sort of 'John Peel' character in his younger days, only his passion was for working Lakeland terriers, rather than hounds.

Ruth tells another tale of a time when Gary bought a cow in order to provide his family with fresh milk daily. The cow needed milking twice a day, but very often Gary couldn't get back in time to do the job, for he was either working, or was out digging.

On these occasions a friend called Neil would help out and would come and milk the cow, but, said Ruth, she was rather bad tempered and often kicked the bucket of milk, as well as Neil himself, over. Many a time he emerged from milking having been badly kicked by that belligerent bovine!

Gary is convinced that two of his Lakeland terriers once saved his life. He was out hunting and was crossing a fell with his coupled terriers, Rags and Judy, a chocolate bitch, by his side, when two horses began approaching him.

The stallion was rather wild and was obviously intent on attacking Gary, who, scanning the wide-open, bleak and barren fell, had nowhere to go. Knowing that he was in trouble, he loosed the two terriers, in the hopes that they would not abandon him and run the other way.

The aggression of the horse sparked something in the terriers and they attacked the stallion, with Judy grabbing it by the nose and Rags hanging on elsewhere. The fire went quickly out of the stallion and Gary watched as it ran and attempted to shake off the determined pair of terriers. It eventually succeeded and the two dogs returned to their master shortly afterwards. Middleton believes that, had the terriers not attacked, then he would probably have been killed by that horse.

Anyone who doubts this should see a stallion intent on mischief. I was out with two of my terriers, Rock and Ghyll, when a Clydesdale stallion; a massive beast with feet the size of dustbin lids, charged at us. I was on the other side of the barbed fence, so was safe, but the two terriers were in the same field as the horse. I quickly called them out, however, when that horse attempted to kick and stamp on them. So I can well believe that Gary's fears were well founded and that that brace of terriers undoubtedly saved his life.

Gary often went digging with a farmer friend of his, Freddie Downham, who farmed near Kendal. They were called out to deal with a marauding fox one springtime and were heading across a fell near Windermere, intent on checking a drain among some rushes where a litter of cubs was residing. As they were searching among the rush beds, a calf jumped out of the undergrowth and bellowed to its mother, for the fellside also contained a large herd of beef cattle. The mother then came rushing over and looked similar in attitude to that wild stallion Middleton had encountered on an earlier occasion. However, Freddie was a farmer and knew about stock, so he told Gary to see off the cow, who, by now, had been joined by much of the herd. However, instead of backing away when Gary attempted to see it off, the cow charged instead, which is not a good sign! Middleton and Freddie Downham, realising they were in trouble, with a large herd of beef cattle intent on splattering them across the fellside, then made a run for it, to the only tree in the immediate vicinity; a hawthorn bush which had grown to a considerable size.

Gary described his climb up that tree, with a brace of coupled terriers to hold onto, as 'not easy', but what was worse was that they were then stuck up that tree for the next three hours, while the herd remained below, hoping their quarry would come down! Eventually the herd lost interest and they steadily drifted away, which gave the pair of would-be hunters' opportunity to descend and flee as quickly as possible. Middleton says there was a large Hereford bull on that fell with the herd, but that he gave them no problems. It was obviously the bellowing calf that sparked the protective instinct in the mother and the rest of the herd. Gary then finished his tale by saying that a number of people have been killed in the Lakes by herds of beef cattle.

Gary was out with the Lunesdale Foxhounds many years ago, when John Nicholson was still the Huntsman. They had hunted a fox for some distance when, near Brough; one of the wildest districts in the north of England, their quarry went to ground inside a large scree-bed, which Gary says is a very bad place. One of the followers was Middleton's gamekeeper friend mentioned earlier and Gary says he was rather loud and a bit of a show-off. He was known to have a good terrier or two though (most of which were Middleton, or part-Middleton bred), and so was asked to try his earth dog, Paddy. Paddy entered a large hole that was big enough for the keeper to squeeze into, while he listened for his terrier signalling a 'find', his 'builders' bum' sticking out of the rocks.

By now quite a number of followers had gathered and they awaited the unfolding events as they stood around that rockpile. And then the terrierman began a loud running commentary of what was going on inside that earth. "He's at it now, oh he's got it, he's killin''it now. He'll fettle it afore long, will Paddy." He shouted, for all to hear, but soon stifled giggles began to spread among the expectant crowd, giggles that grew into often uncontrollable laughter as the keeper continued with his ramblings. Until, that is, he emerged from out of that mini cave in order to see what all the fuss was about; what exactly was so amusing. And that is when he saw Paddy, stood on the top of those rocks and looking down at his owner, wagging his stumpy tail at the sound of his masters' voice; his triumphant utterances as he commentated on how hard his dog was at the fox!

Terriers can be a source of great embarrassment, as we have just seen, and Middleton once dug to a dog called Rambo, not of his breeding he was quick to stress, that was barking at a small hole into which a mouse must have run, for it was too narrow to allow a rat access. It had taken a hard four or five-foot dig to discover this and the lads were not happy at all, though the owner wasn't too pleased either!

A few years ago Gary was contacted by a keen hunter from Ontario in Canada and he asked if Middleton could send him a couple of his Lakeland terriers for racoon hunting. Racoon hounds were used for the actual hunting of these beasts, which can be rather a nuisance and, like foxes, will prey on chickens and suchlike, but it was his Jack Russell terriers that were used whenever they got into almost inaccessible places. If they could be dug out, the Russells, being more traditional sorts that would stand off and bay, were ideal for this job, but this chap was having to leave many racoons simply because they were getting into large bales from where they could not be reached. The Jack Russells would find their quarry and bay at it, but the racoons soon grew wise to this and they began attacking the terriers and driving them out, for they knew they would not tackle them. Hence the reason why this Canadian hunter wanted something harder.

When I first started with terriers, I worked Jack Russells and found them to be very game little dogs; ideal for digging out foxes, or for bolting those that would bolt, but I found them rather lacking when a fox would not shift from an earth that was virtually impossible to dig. True, they would stay and bay, nip and tease, and sometimes succeed in persuading a fox to bolt, but very often the fox had to be left and when this was a lamb, or chicken stealing fox, then it was hard to stomach, especially for the farmer. Hence the reason why I started up in Fell, or Lakeland terriers, all those years ago.

It was the same situation for this chap. He was having to leave racoons alive and well and this just wasn't good enough, so he rang Middleton and Gary sent him two adult black and tan Lakelands that he had already entered and both had proven hard fox killing terriers. They arrived safely in Canada and it wasn't long before Gary received a phone call, which told of how they were progressing. They entered to racoon without any problems. After hunting them with hounds, they had got into the bales as usual and were undoubtedly expecting the Russells to arrive soon, whom they knew would not attack and so they prepared to drive them out once more. However, they soon received quite a shock, for the black and tan Lakelands entered, took an initial bite or two, and then erupted, killing their quarry quickly and efficiently and thus solving the problem of how to deal with those racoons that got out of reach of hounds.

The black and tan terriers featured on the video, *Johnny D' & The Black and Tans*, were purchased from Gary when the subject of this famous ratting video bought a bitch and her litter from him. The Middleton strain of Lakeland terrier has proven game to all types of quarry, from rats to racoons to badgers.

Gary has not only owned some excellent foxing lurchers, but he has worked with quite a few that belonged to hunting companions. He was out hunting near Leeds and Tim, one of Middleton's best terriers, was entered into quite a bad place at a scrapyard. The fox, finding the terrier a little too hot to handle, finally bolted and came running from between two skips. His companion owned a Hancock bred lurcher (Gary has seen 4 or 5 Hancock lurchers at work and has been most impressed with their capabilities) that looked like a sheepdog, but it was a cracking fox catching lurcher and quickly caught and killed the fox Tim had bolted. Middleton has seen some excellent bull terrier bred lurchers at work to fox and has also been very impressed with these, although, he says, they do not have the brains of the Hancock dogs.

Many years ago, during the early days of Middleton's breeding programme, he was out hunting along the river Gowan, near Staveley, with his bitch, Nettle, when she entered a stone drain that she found close to the river. Nettle scrambled up the long stone pipe for quite some distance and then pandemonium broke out, with the terrier baying and screaming with rage. A few minutes later a large otter bolted from the pipe and ran for the river. Nettle wasn't far behind and Gary then enjoyed an exciting hunt for the next fifteen, or twenty minutes, as Nettle followed her quarry downstream, until scent could no longer be held.

Middleton had been out digging for much of the day around the Mallerstang district which was once the haunt of the late Cyril Breay (where he and his father established a hard working strain of terrier by crossing fell terriers with their Sealyham terriers that they had brought with them from south Wales, terriers they used for fox and badger digging, as both were passionate badger diggers during those early days), and they had finally succeeded in accounting for a badger which had been placed in a sack for release elsewhere, according to the wishes of the farmer. On the way back, as was customary in those days, they decided to stop off at a hostelry, where much-needed refreshments were to be enjoyed. This was many years ago when badger digging was not frowned upon as it is now; the image ruined by louts who bait, rather than dig and deal humanely with, their quarry.

There is a massive difference 'twixt badger digging and badger baiting and folk like Middleton have always treated their quarry humanely, usually releasing their captives into long disused setts. Gary and friends now stood outside a pub in Hawes; a charming Wensleydale market town, with 'Brock' secured inside a sack slung over his shoulder.

A chap then asked what was in the sack and Gary told him, with the enquirer asking if he could take a photograph of the animal, for he had never seen one before. Middleton agreed and managed to get the badger by the tail, pulling it free of the sack. The chap, having taken his photo, then asked if he could hold the beast. Again, Gary agreed, telling him to wait until he could get the tail, but he was a little impatient and grabbed hold of the back leg instead, the badger swinging round and biting him through the hand. His fascination, said Gary, soon melted away, for the crushing bite of a badger is one no sane person would wish to experience!

The blue and fawn bitch, Nettle, was an incredibly game terrier and Gary worked her hard for a few seasons, bred some good litters from her and then sold her in order to make room for younger stuff. He has never had any problems finding buyers for his terriers and never needs to resort to advertising (demand far outstrips supply), but Nettle was keenly snapped up when she became available. Middleton was out with Brian Longstaff of Newcastle when she was entered into a bad place that wasn't usually dug, but the bitch engaged her quarry and a dig was thus necessary. The going was incredibly difficult and it took all day to reach the bitch and her quarry, but she had never flinched in all that time and had stayed until she was finally dug out. Brian offered Gary twenty-five pounds for Nettle, which was a large amount in those days, and he accepted. The bloodlines of this bitch continue to run strong in the Middleton strain of Lakeland to this day, through, among others, the very game dog, Nailer.

Middleton did much digging with Gary Hallet of Bradford at one time and he said that Hallet was a very good fox-hunter who had a knack of catching this quarry, even among the urban districts of west Yorkshire towns such as Bradford and Leeds. Hallet took Middleton down Thornton road in Bradford and they pulled up near a bus stop. Twenty or so yards from this bus stop was a hole in the wall, and it may still be there today (this was twenty years ago), and Hallet told Middleton to put his terrier into that hole. He did and shortly afterwards there was a racket under a flag by the bus stop, where three old ladies now stood, looking rather puzzled. Middleton then lifted the flag and there was the dog and fox in mortal combat. Gary

Hallet had dug a fox from here on an earlier occasion and had left the hole open and just covered it with the flag, having taken quite a few from this spot ever since. It was one of the easiest hunts Gary has ever taken part in.

Out hunting with Gary Hallet again, Middleton loosed three or four of his terriers into a scrapyard in Leeds that was known to hold a fox or two. Gary states that this yard was full of scrap and the heaps of twisted metal were piled high. There had been a two-inch snowfall during that Saturday night and fox prints were everywhere. The terriers entered the piles of scrap eagerly and their barks, grunts and growls soon indicated that they had found. Shortly afterwards a fox bolted, but simply slipped into another part of the scrap and easily escaped the lurcher. Gary says that six foxes were found in the scrap and all six continued bolting and re-entering the metal piles, or they gave the terriers the run around deep inside. Those game and determined terriers worked those foxes relentlessly for the next three hours and bolted their foxes several times, but they would not leave the scrap and Middleton stated that it was similar to waiting outside while a terrier chased its fox all over a vast borran, unable to catch up with it in order to finish it below ground, and unable to put enough pressure on to evict the tenant from such a huge place. In the end they were forced to leave the foxes, grabbing the terriers one by one as they emerged in order to seek another route to their quarry.

Again in the districts of west Yorkshire, Gary loosed his black and tan dog, Moss; a very typey terrier and one that could easily kill a reluctant fox. I tried to persuade Gary to sell me this terrier a few years ago, but he refused. Moss went eagerly into this pipe and then proceeded to bolt seven foxes, one after another, from this long drain; possibly a record for the number of foxes found inside one earth (outside of the breeding season)!

On another occasion he had a terrier to ground on the outskirts of Bradford and a cricket match was going on nearby. A fox finally bolted and escaped, making its way right through the field of cricketers. Gary stated that they hardly flinched, they must have been that familiar with foxes knocking about the place, saying that a fox running through such a district in the Lakes would cause a sensation. Foxes in the fells, he believes, are far more shy and go out of their way to avoid human habitation, though he once took part in a hunt with the Ullswater Foxhounds that ended when the fox ran through the village of Patterdale and sought sanctuary inside the school. The fox was evicted and finally caught by hounds.

After a hunt up in the Dales with the Lunesdale Foxhounds, Gary ended up back at a hotel in Hawes where a long drinking session started. They all ended up back at Maurice Bell's place (this was before Maurice had set up his Wensleydale pack, when he regularly hunted with the Lunesdale), with John Nicholson rather worse for wear, still decked out in his hunting gear. He fell asleep in a chair, exhausted after a hard hunt and a few drinks, and that is when the mischief began. They raided Mrs Bell's make-up bag and put lipstick on and all sorts all over 'Nic's' face, not letting on when he woke and struggling to stifle the laughter. They all then went off to a hunt social that evening and Nicholson had failed to check his appearance in the mirror. There was great amusement at the social gathering and 'Nic' was advised to 'tek a look in t'mirror.' Taking it rather badly, he chased his Whipper-in, John Dixon, all over the hotel, vowing to 'murder 'im.' Middleton had Rags with him that day and he jumped up and pulled a fox mask off the wall of the hotel.

At the hunt ball of the Lunesdale Foxhounds, John Nicholson went for a drink at the bar and Middleton got up to more mischief. A farmers' wife had won a large steak in the raffle and, while she was dancing and 'Nic' was at the bar, Gary, watched by his companion, Ken Harrison, put the steak inside Nicholson's coat pocket, which he had hung on a nearby chair. The lady returned soon afterwards and went mad, saying someone had stolen her steak. It was later discovered in 'Nic's' pocket and things had become so heated that Middleton slunk away, leaving them to sort it out as Nicholson was accused of stealing the meat!

Gary once raised two badger cubs that he had dug from a sett and he eventually gave them to Frank Stacey of the Holme Valley Beagles. Frank had some useful terriers that were game to fox and Barry Wild, while establishing his own strain of working Lakeland, used Stacey stud dogs. Frank and Sheila, his wife, actually kept these two badgers in a spare bedroom, inside a sort of artificial sett, but they dug through the wall, as well as causing other damage, and so they ended up putting them into a sett outside. Middleton cannot remember what happened to them after this, but one can assume that they quickly turned wild and forsook their human companions. With all of the countryside around Holmfirth, they would not have had a problem finding a suitable home.

Rags, the son of Rex, was one of the hardest terriers Middleton has owned and he took many foxes and badgers using this dog. If a fox did not get out of there fairly rapidly, then it was certain to die in its lair when Rags was entered. And so Gary was rather puzzled one day when, after entering an

Diane Barker with descendant of Rock. The ghyll to her left is where Barker's Rock ran to meet hounds marking to ground, then finishing his quarry below ground.

A mounted fox taken with Fred Barker's Pennine pack at Ousby.
Maybe his 'Chowt-faced' Rock worked this fox!

My bitch, Mist, a hard terrier with plenty of Middleton bloodlines.

My dog, Fell, descended from Middleton's Ben, marking mink under a large rock.

Neil Wilson's Alfie killing a mink. Alfie is out of Fell and Mist (ph. Neil Wilson).

A mink taken using Alfie (ph. Neil Wilson).

earth in the Lythe valley, Rags began baying rather vociferously, which, to say the least, was more than a little unusual. Middleton dug to his dog and finally uncovered his terrier, which was still baying strongly. After clearing a space around the terrier and pulling him back a little, Gary discovered the reason for Rags' unusual behaviour; a shelduck sitting on its nest. Gary remarked that Rags killed foxes for fun, quickly and efficiently in similar fashion to his sire and grandsire, but he would not go near the duck, which, to the dog, was a very unusual find indeed. The same thing happened to Derek Webster when hunting a keepered spot in Cheshire. He dug down to a border terrier that was baying strongly and he too uncovered a shelduck on a nest.

Gary has often hunted with the Kendal and District Otterhounds and he would run his terriers loose on the bank, while hounds drew the river. One day, at Pooley Bridge, an otter was found and Gary watched as hounds swam for quite some distance out onto the lake in pursuit of their quarry. On another occasion, while drawing the riverbank, Gary came across a mink in a trap. Hounds had moved on and Middleton decided to dispatch the quarry quickly, using Rags. They loosed the mink out in the field and it flew at Gary's friend, Tony Birkett, before making a run for it. Rags was loosed and went after his quarry eagerly, but Gary said that the mink bit the dog several times all over his face before it finally perished. Mink are very aggressive fighters and it takes a game terrier to tackle one. A dog I bred, Alfie, owned by Neil Wilson, a one-time follower of the Lunesdale Foxhounds, and possessing several lines back to Middleton's dogs, has taken many mink and is proving a game terrier indeed.

Diane Barker, the daughter of Anthony, has continued breeding her father's and grandfather's strain of terrier when she took a Cowen bred bitch to a grandson of Wilk's Rock, also named Rock, over twenty years ago, a terrier owned by Sid Wilkinson in his latter years. She has bred some good terriers from this line, one of which is a dog called Rock who has served for two seasons with the Coniston Foxhounds. Diane lost one of her bitches, Judy, out on the fell while gathering sheep. This terrier self-entered and simply disappeared. Diane can only surmise, and correctly in my opinion, that the bitch went to ground in a borran, many of which litter the fellsides close to the Barker farmstead, and either became trapped, or, more than likely, was killed by badger. Diane has recently bred a chocolate coloured puppy with a couple of white paws and a bit of white on its chest; a terrier that confirms she is still breeding the line of terrier bred down from Fred Barker's strain. This chocolate colouring entered the strain after a spaniel/fell terrier cross was mated to 'Chowt-faced' Rock. While on the subject of Fred Barker's Rock, I would like to explain that the Middleton strain is also descended from this dog via Arthur Irving's Robin – a superb worker that saw much service with the Eskdale and Ennerdale Foxhounds. A terrier named Grip, having served the Ullswater Foxhounds well during Bowman's latter years (he once killed two foxes in one day's hunting) and having been given to Harold Watson on Bowman's retirement, was mated to Gyp, a terrier sired by 'Chowt-faced' Rock, and this union produced Fury. Anthony Chapman's Crab, a famous Coniston terrier, mated Fury and this resulted in Peggy. Peggy was mated by Rastus and bred Grip, a terrier eventually killed by badger. Grip mated Joe Wilkinson's Nettle and produced Towser, a terrier that went to Willie Irving at the Melbreak and a dog who became the grandsire of Irving's famous Turk (1930s); one of the hardest terriers ever to work with a fellpack and an ancestor of Arthur's Robin. And so the Middleton strain carries several lines back to 'Chowt-faced' Rock; the dog who first produced the magnificent heads for which Middleton's strain is now famous.

Chipper Smith, writer for *Earth Dog, Running Dog*, has much respect for Gary Middleton and he has had some good stuff out of the Middleton strain, which he has crossed with Parkes' stuff, producing some excellent workers that he uses both above and below ground. Chipper remarked that he has never seen terriers enter to fox has quickly as do Middleton strain Lakelands. One of the best Chipper has seen at work is a dog called Barney which belongs to a hunting companion, a dog bought from Hemel Hempstead and bred out of Middleton/Brightmore (Buck/Breay/Middleton) stuff. As I explained earlier in the book, there are many digging lads on the outskirts of London who use and breed Middleton strain working terriers. Many of these are very game and typey, but they are never seen at shows, for these lads are keen diggers and do not bother with shows and showing. Middleton has purposely sold many terriers to such individuals in order to ensure less competition in the showring.

Kenny McCallister of Scotland has several Middleton and part Middleton bred terriers which he uses for fox digging and bolting, though he states that, if he wishes for a fox to be bolted, he will not use pure Middleton terriers, not the dogs anyway, for they will allow few to bolt. He has some descended from Tyke and Twist, the sons of Toby who were also part Ward bred, and others half Middleton/Tyson bred, and these are generally not as hard as pure Middleton stuff, though they are by no means 'softies' and some are fox killers. His pure stuff is mainly bred out of Middleton's Chad, a dog bred by Gary, but actually belonging to Sue Middleton, and one that closely resembles Wilk's Rock. Chad has a superb head, as do his sons, but Middleton told me that Wilk's Rock had an even better head, which gives you some idea of how good a dog Rock was.

Wayne Hill of Bolton also uses and breeds Middleton stuff. His best dog was Tiger, a red dog with a massive head and general good type, but an excellent worker who made quite a name for himself in the north, as well as in Somerset where Wayne has dug quite a bit of stuff with his terriers. Tiger was such a good looking and working dog that Kenny McCallister was intent on using Tiger to bring into his own breeding programme, but then tragedy struck. Wayne's son entered the dog into a large earth, mainly made up of ash, and the terrier engaged his fox thirty feet from the entrance at a depth of fifteen feet. Wayne arrived later and digging commenced. The mark on the locator was exact throughout and Wayne thought this a little unusual, as there was usually some amount of movement, however slight. So for the last five feet he was convinced Tiger was dead. His assumption sadly proved correct and Wayne uncovered his dead terrier, which had dug onto his fox and had thus suffocated in the tight space.

He has a few Middleton bred terriers and one of the best he has seen is Abe, a brother to his black and tan bitch, a terrier that is much used for fox digging. He has recently purchased Moses from Andrew Meeks, a terrier bred out of Sam, the son of Middleton's Rex. Abe has sired another grand worker, Spike, who is a fox killer and will allow few to bolt. The very day on which I spoke to Wayne over the phone, Abe had been to a fox in a large rockpile and had taken quite a mauling. Wayne has done very well in the showring with his dogs and has won several times, some with Tiger before his demise. I once saw this terrier at a show and was most impressed with the magnificent head on this dog; a head typical of Rock's offspring. One of the easiest digs he ever took part in was with Tiger. The terrier entered and soon settled, engaging his fox and tackling it hard until Wayne dug him out at a depth of just eight inches.

The hardiness and working ability of the Middleton strain has been demonstrated throughout each successive generation and the strain continues to produce top class workers. Trixie was one of Middleton's best bitches and he remembers a hard dig in the Lythe valley after he had entered her into a peat earth – a typically bad place where even the most vociferous of terriers could not be heard. Trixie stuck with her quarry until Gary finally reached her two days later. This strain of working Lakeland terrier has been fully tested both in the showring and, more importantly, in the field. And it hasn't been found wanting!

Postscript:

We had all been out for a meal at a local hotel and had then returned to Gary and Ruth Middleton's house; a charming old stone farmhouse, in order to enjoy a 'wee dram' in front of the roaring open fire. The ladies had gone up to bed and Gary and I chatted for some time, the subject, of course, turning chiefly to hounds, terriers and hunting in general. Gary then summed up all that he admired in a working terrier and I could do little else but agree with his sentiments. "When a terrier will walk for miles o'er windswept fells in t'middle o' winter, a howling gale ragin' across the bleak landscape, following in the wake of hounds. And then will sit by an earth on Shap fell until t'fox has 'drubbed' a terrier or two sent in to shift it, having to endure often terrible conditions, before it gets a chance of work. Then it enters t'earth and engages its quarry, either bolting it, killing it below, or staying until dug out. That's when yuh can say a terrier is game!" It was obvious to me that his sentiments were borne of experience; an experience of hunting that bleak and inhospitable landscape known as the English Lake District.

Barry Wild has used Middleton blood to produce hard fox dogs and show winners.

Barry Wild's red dog, a hard terrier to fox.

Gary with Nailer; a very game terrier used by George Newcombe on his Bedlington strain.

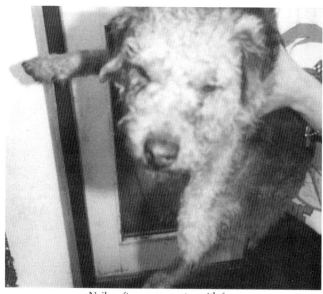

Nailer after an encounter with fox.

Billy – as game as they come.

Chad winning champion of champions at Midland Game Fair '97 –
breeder of game and good looking stock.

Tarzan at eleven months – already entered to fox.

Jock – sire of Nailer and used by Bill Brightmore on his bitches.

Trixie watching a dig. A daughter of Tim.

A lovely bitch, Tanner.

Neil Hannam of Wales with his working Middleton bred bitch, Judy.

A chocolate pup bred by Diane Barker in '05. This colour was first introduced to this strain when 'Chowt-faced' Rock mated a spaniel/fell cross belonging to Anthony Pool back in the 1920s.

Jed, a hard terrier which served at the North Lonsdale Foxhounds.

Punch, a four month old pup out of Rex, bred late '05 and displaying breeding remains true to type decades on since Wilk's Rock (ph. Pauline Middleton).

Another view of Punch. Note the tight, iron-hard jacket and good strong head (ph. Pauline Middleton).

Barney, belongs to Andrew Peacock, Chipper Smith's hunting companion, is a superb worker. For his first dig on trial he found a fox in a vast earth and stayed six hours until dug out (ph. Chipper Smith).

Gem (left), a daughter of Barney, and Willow, Chipper's Parkes bred bitch (ph. Chipper Smith).

Bob, out of Andrew Meeks Sam, is a grandson of Middleton's Rex
and is owned by Kenny McCallister.

Bob and Bonnie. Bonnie is out of Meg, purchased from Gary Middleton
and owned by Kenny McCallister.

Bloodlines of Some Middleton Strain Lakeland Terriers:

Wilkinson's Rock was put to Trixie (red) and produced Rex. Rex mated Judy, the Welsh terrier bitch, and produced Judy 2. Rex later mated his own daughter, Judy 2, and produced Rex 2. Rex 2 mated Tanner and the result was Toby. Toby was put to Trixie (black & tan) and this resulted in Rex 3, Middleton's current stud dog who is a veteran of ten years and is on the front cover of this book. Rex 3 has bred many useful workers and lookers (this is just one line that goes back to Wilk's Rock, though there are many, many others).

Rex, the son of Wilk's Rock, mated Candy and bred Jock. Jock was put to Nettle, a very game bitch, and this resulted in Nailer, the dog used by George Newcombe to 'spice up' his strain of working Bedlingtons.

Old Rex mated Ken James' bitch, Floss, and produced Flint and Gravel. Gravel was mated to Becky and bred Billy. From Billy came a dynasty of top winning and working Jack Russell types.

Old Rex mated Jewel, a daughter of Trixie and a superb fox-killing bitch, and this union produced Tanner. Rex 2 then mated Tanner and bred Toby, the sire of, among many others, Tyke, Twist and Rusty.

The sire of Boss, the terrier which recently entered at just ten months, is Rex 3, when put to a bitch bred out of Jake, a dog sired by Rusty, the son of Toby. The red dog, Punch, bred by Bob and Ruth Arnold and now at Gary's kennels, is bred exactly the same way, but from a later mating.

Photo Captions: (some photos are of poor quality, but are included because of their importance to this record).

1. P.6(T) Chip, looker and worker, the subject of our introduction.
2. P.6(B) Rusty, a Middleton bred Lakeland and Sire of Chad.
3. P.7(T) A son of Chad.
4. P.7(B) A son of Toby.
5. P.17(T) Fred Barker with terriers and badger dug using 'Chowt-faced' Rock. This trio of terriers founded the strain that was later continued by Gary Middleton.
6. P.17(B) Young Anthony Barker with Ilfracombe terriers and a hound from the Pennine pack at Ousby.
7. P.18(T) Diane Barker with a terrier descended from her father's, and grandfather's, strain.
8. P.18(B) Diane Barker's fell bitch, similar in type to Barker's Rock.

9. P.28(T) Trouble, an improved terrier from the Dent, Wilk's Rock strain.
10. P.28(B) Rusty, out of Toby and a top winning terrier.
11. P.33(T) Sid Wilkinson's Jenny, 1948, a grandam of Rock.
12. P.33(B) Crippin and Tim, vastly improved in type and working ability, out of Chip and Judy.
13. P.34(T) Trixie, out of Wilk's Rock and dam of old Rex.
14. P.34(B) Jewel, daughter of Trixie and Chip.
15. P.37(T) A working Lakeland, Tim.
16. P.37(B) Rags, the son of old Rex, and Jed, the near-black terrier, who served at the North Lonsdale Foxhounds and was used to finish reluctant foxes.
17. P.38(T) Tim and Jed with Jack, a good foxing lurcher.
18. P.38(B) A dig at Kirkby Lonsdale. L-R: John Bell, Jackie Robinson, Gary Middleton, Jakey Howard and Arthur Wells.
19. P.39(T) Hoot.
20. P.39(B) Nettle, a veteran at eight years (Gary dug five badgers in one day using this bitch).
21. P.40(T) Candy.
22. P.40(B) Spike, out of Wilk's Jock. He entered on his first dig when Gary took two badgers with him.
23. P.41(T) Tim, out of Rock (one of the terriers returned to Sid Wilk's and passed on to Gary).
24. P.41(B) Rusty, loaned to keeper who sent it to Bramham Moor Hunt.
25. P.42(T) Rex, son of old Rex. This terrier has a head similar to Fred Barker's Rock.
26. P.42(B) Rex, Nettle and Punch. Punch worked with hill pack in Wales.
27. P.59(T) Middleton and Brian Fleming with Bracken, Ben and fox taken that day.
28. P.59(B) Middleton and friends at sett at Witherslack. Group includes Malcolm Lambert and Dave Roberts.
29. P60(T) Chad as a pup.
30. P.60(B) Jessie and Sparky, sired by Punch who worked in Wales.
31. P.61(T) Whiskey, bought by Brian Meeks, a type very similar to Wilk's Rock.
32. P.61(B) A good typey terrier bought by Bob and Ruth Arnold.
33. P.62(T) Trixie drawing 'Brock' at the end of the dig (Winster valley).
34. P.62(B) Middleton Lakelands popularly known as Johnny D's black and tans.
35. P.71(T) Daughter of Sid Wilkinson's Jock with litter bred early 80s (ph. Bob and Ruth Arnold).
36. P.71(B) Bill Brightmore with terrier improved by using Middleton bloodlines.
37. P.72(T) Rex, sold to Brian Meeks, entered to first fox and drew it from the earth.
38. P.72(B) Tim – a very game terrier.
39. P.73(T) Judy winning East Lancashire show.
40. P.73(B) Lucky – superb foxing lurcher.
41. P.74(T) A terrier sold to Ireland where many Middleton strain Lakelands are at work.
42. P.74(B) Punch, early 90s. I saw this self-entering terrier at work (ph. Bob and Ruth Arnold).
43. P.79(T) P. 79-86 show before, stripping and after shots, and tools used.
44. P.79(B).
45. P.80(T).
46. P.80(B).
47. P.81(T).
48. P.81(B).
49. P.82(T).
50. P.82(B).
51. P.83(T).
52. P.83(B).
53. P.84(T).
54. P.84(B).
55. P.85(T).
56. P.85(B).
57. P.86(T).
58. P.86(B).

59. P.91(T) Rex and his son Boss, who entered to and killed first fox at ten months (ph. Bob and Ruth Arnold).
60. P.91(B) The red dog winning Lowther, before heading off to Scotland (ph. Bob and Ruth Arnold).
61. P.92(T) After winning champion pup at Lowther '05, this red dog entered to its first fox during a dig in Scotland (ph. Pauline Middleton).
62. P.92(B) Toby, looker and worker and sire of Desie Makin's Tyke and Neil Stobbart's Twist.
63. P.93(T) Hoot, a game terrier, but with the poor blue and fawn colouring.
64. P.93(B) Rex at Lowther '99, very game, typey and with good colour.
65. P.97(T) Lookers and workers, Middleton's terriers with dead fox.
66. P.97(B) Trouble, looker and worker. She won this Welsh show three years running.
67. P.98(T) Becky, daughter of Rex (Aug '05). The influence of Wilkinson's Rock can clearly be seen all these years later (ph. Bob and Ruth Arnold).
68. P.98(B) Boss, son of Rex and hard terrier (ph. Bob and Ruth Arnold).
69. P.99(T) p.99-100 – just some of the trophies won by Middleton's terriers.
70. P.99(B)
71. P.100(T)
72. P.100(B)
73. P.101(T) Just some of the rosettes won by Middleton's terriers.
74. P.101(B) Thousands of rosettes, though there were more.
75. P.102(T) Middleton with rosettes piled almost to his elbow.
76. P.102(B) Rex, a veteran at ten years, but still game and typey.
77. P.114(T) Mist, of good type due to Middleton blood.
78. P.114(B) Mist, winner of her class.
79. P.115(T) Beck, daughter of Mist; another winner.
80. P.115(B) Barry Wild with his very typey black and tan dog, improved using Middleton blood. Barry's terriers are also excellent workers.
81. P.116(T) A middleton bred pup similar in type to Wilk's Rock, a result of line breeding over many years.
82. P.116(B) A daughter of Chad and Barry Wild's black bitch.
83. P.117(T) Basher, a looker, but wouldn't enter. Middleton is honest enough to admit when one of his terriers won't work, though non-workers are rare.
84. P.117(B) Rex, nearly lost at Preston (sire: old Rex. Dam: Judy (part Welsh).
85. P.118(T) Granddaughter Yasmin with Mist at a show.
86. P.118(B) Gary and friends digging a fox in the south Lakes.
87. P.119(T) A Bill Brightmore black owned by Seamus Irwin. Put to Rex, this terrier became the ancestor of plenty of smart black stuff.
88. P.119(B) Tim, similar in type to old Rex, his great grandsire.
89. P.130(T) Billy as a puppy.
90. P.130(B) Billy as an adult (ph. Bob and Ruth Arnold).
91. P.131(T) Jed, out of Billy and Nut. Jed went to America working racoons (ph. Bob and Ruth Arnold).
92. P.131(B) Gin at Patterdale show. She was later stolen.
93. P.132(T) A terrier out of Billy at Lowther.
94. P.132(B) Pippa, out of coloured parents Jessie and Punch – the same who worked with hill pack in Wales.
95. P.133(T) A white out of a coloured litter.
96. P.133(B) Frost, out of Billy and Nut (ph. Bob and Ruth Arnold).
97. P.134(T) The white bitch entered at Keighley and killed by badger in Ireland.
98. P.134(B) Old fashioned fox terriers similar in type to today's white Lakelands.
99. P.135 Certificate proving working abilities of Middleton strain. Awarded to Soda.
100. P.136 A second certificate awarded to Soda. These were for digs held on 12/9/93, 6/10/93, 10/10/93 and 11/10/93 in different locations.
101. P.137(T) A red Lakeland with white blaze, betraying fox terrier ancestry.

Terrier hat-trick

Lakeland Terrier breeder Mr Gary Middleton is going from strength to strength this season.

His Lakeland dog Rex won three championships in three shows over the May Bank Holiday weekend.

Rex's daughter Nettle, a bitch puppy, is keeping up the standard with an impressive record of six wins in six show appearances.

And Mr Middleton's bitch Trouble picked up first prize in its class at Llangollen Show. This makes it a hat-trick of wins at the big North Wales show for Mr Middleton, of Bateman Fold Farm, Crook, as in 1985 and 1986 he was awarded the overall championship.

Mr Middleton, a breeder of Lakeland Terriers for 20 years, said: "I have been doing OK for a number of years, but it is a remarkable thing for Rex to win in three days in different areas of the country and with three judges."

Mr Gary Middleton of Bateman Fold pictured with his prize-winning Lakeland terrier bitch Trouble.

Another win for Trouble.
Courtesy of the Westmoreland Gazette.